EASY PIANO

TOP HITS OF 2014

S0-BMU-410

ISBN 978-1-4950-0092-8

HAL•LEONARD®
CORPORATION
7777 W. BLUEMOUND RD. P.O. BOX 13819 MILWAUKEE, WI 53213

Visit Hal Leonard Online at
www.halleonard.com

ALL OF ME

Words and Music by JOHN STEPHENS
and TOBY GAD

Moderately, with feeling

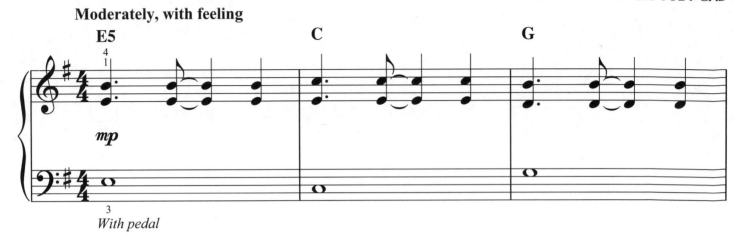

mp

With pedal

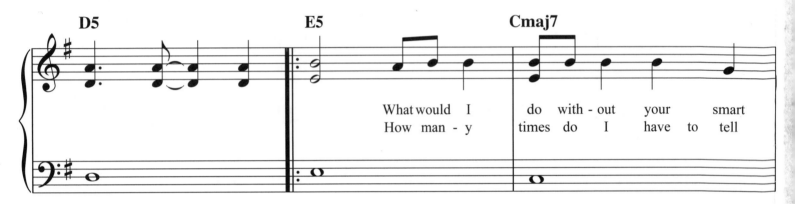

What would I do with-out your smart
How man-y times do I have to tell

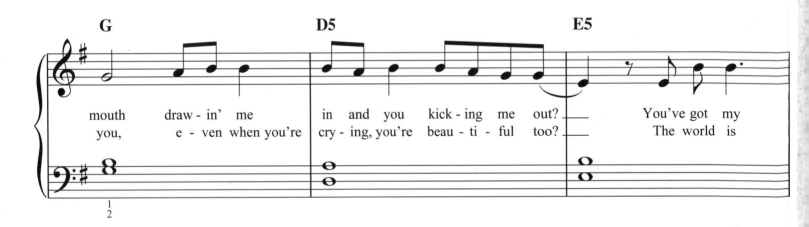

mouth draw-in' me in and you kick-ing me out? You've got my
you, e-ven when you're cry-ing, you're beau-ti-ful too? The world is

head spin-nin', no kid-din'. I can't pin you down.
beat-ing you down. I'm a-round through ev-er-y mood.

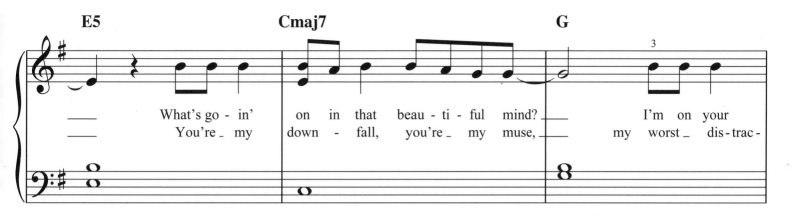

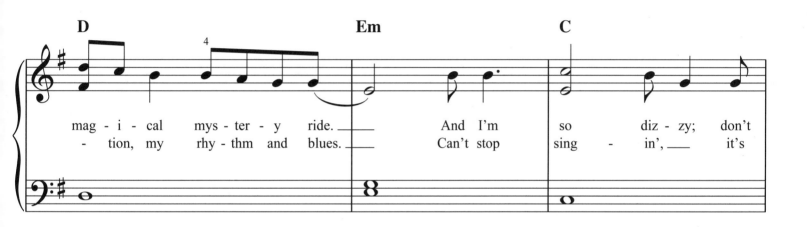

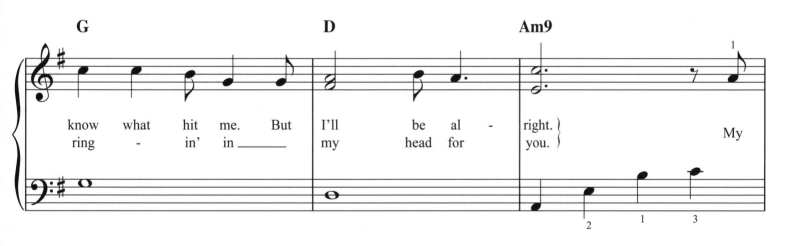

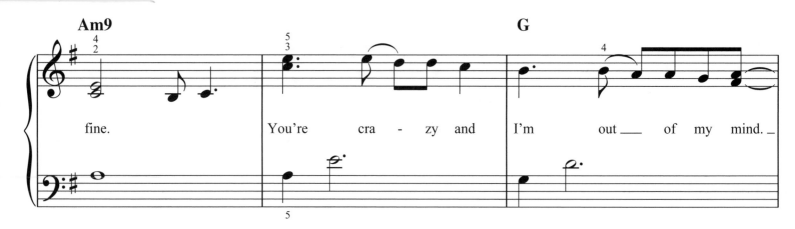

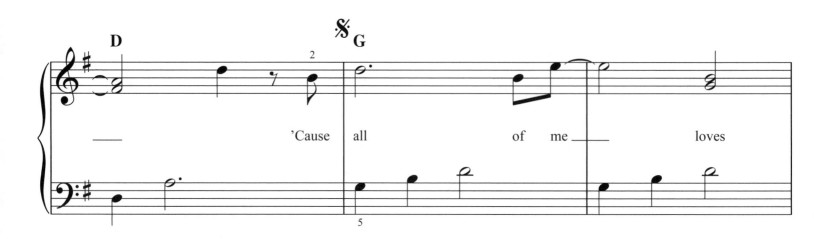

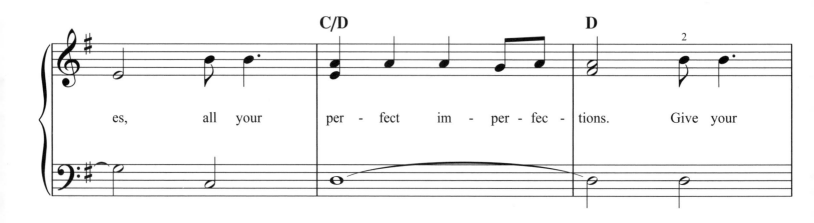

all   to me,   I'll give my   all   to you.

You're my   end and my be - gin - ning.   E - ven

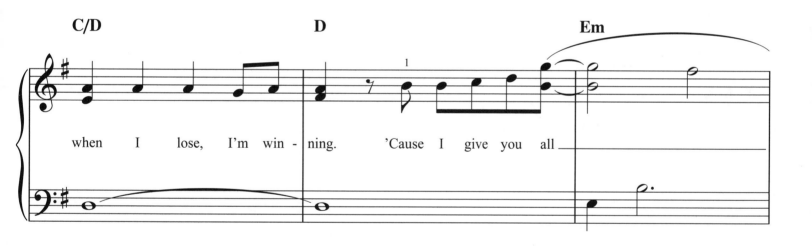

when I lose, I'm win - ning.   'Cause I give you all

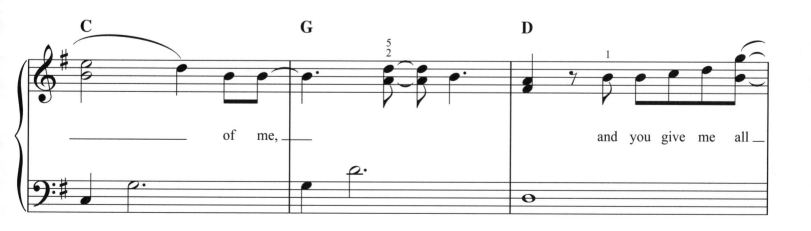

of me,   and you give me all

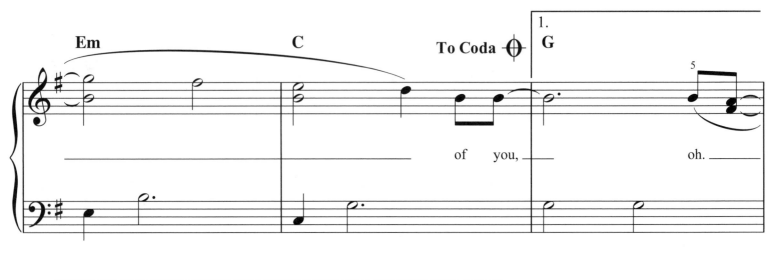

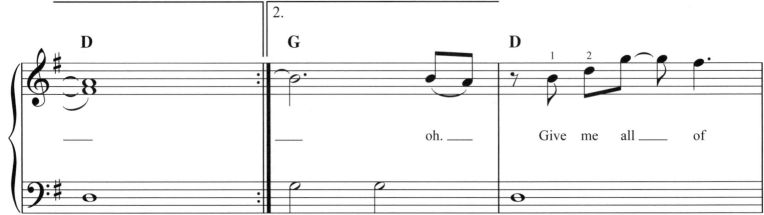

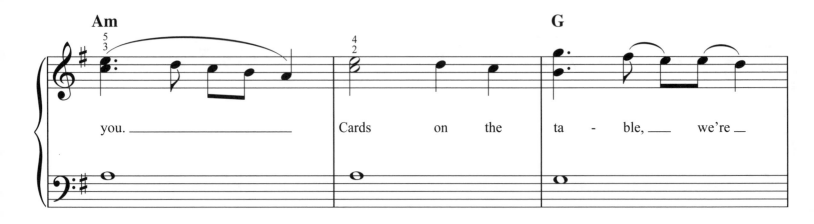

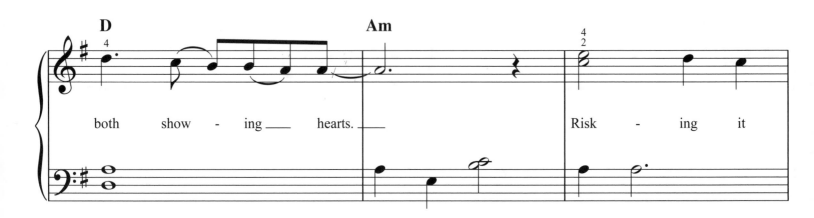

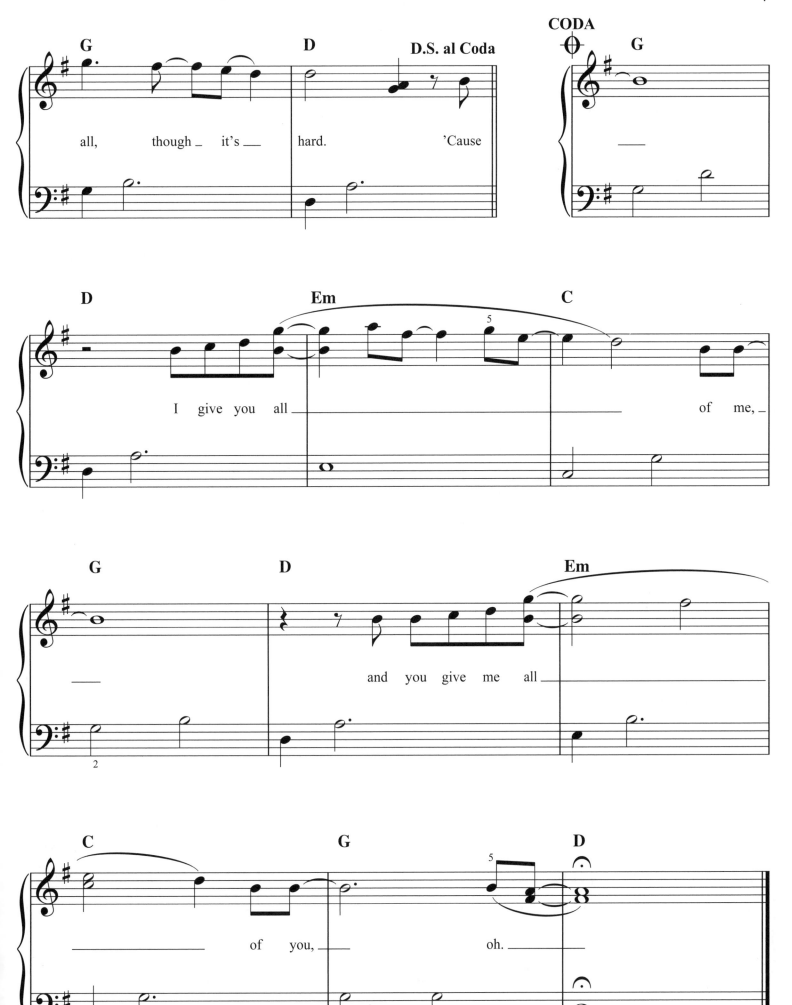

AM I WRONG

Words and Music by VINCENT DERY,
NICOLAY SEREBA, WILLIAM WIIK LARSEN
and ABDOULIE JALLOW

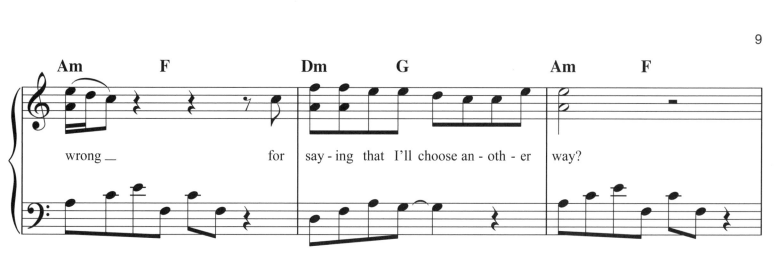

wrong _   for say - ing that I'll choose an - oth - er   way?

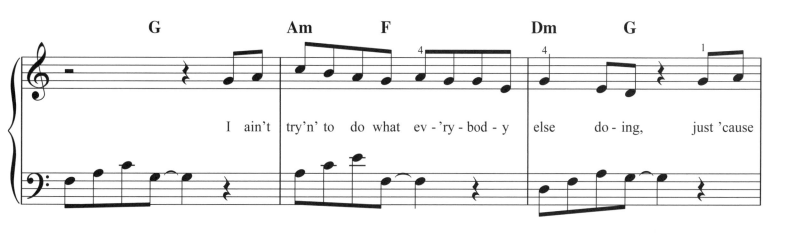

I ain't try'n' to do what ev - 'ry - bod - y else do - ing,   just 'cause

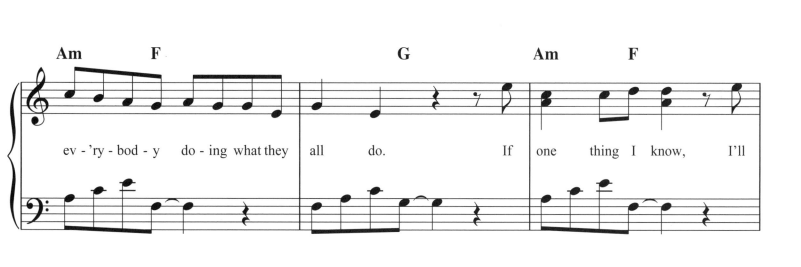

ev - 'ry - bod - y do - ing what they all do.   If one thing I know, I'll

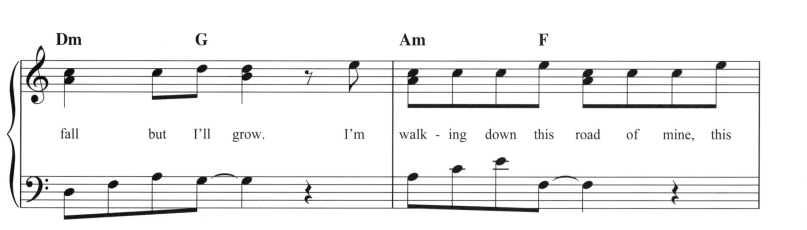

fall   but I'll grow. I'm walk - ing down this road of mine, this

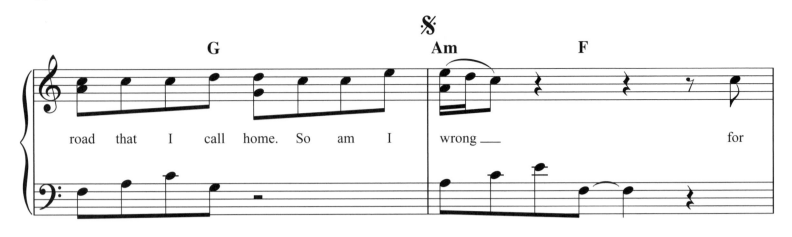

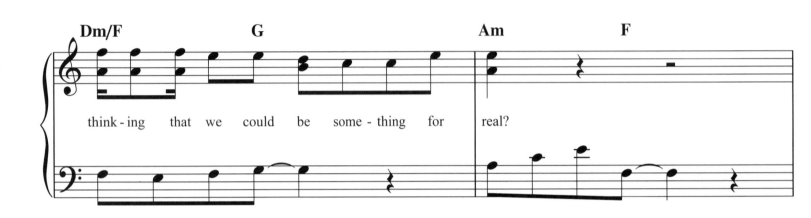

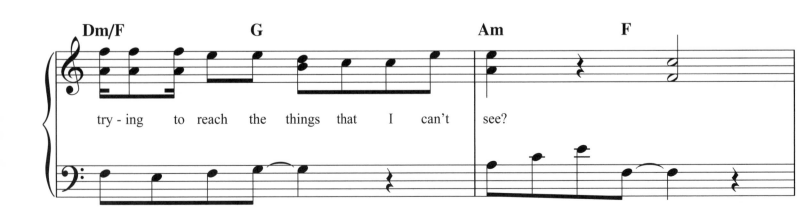

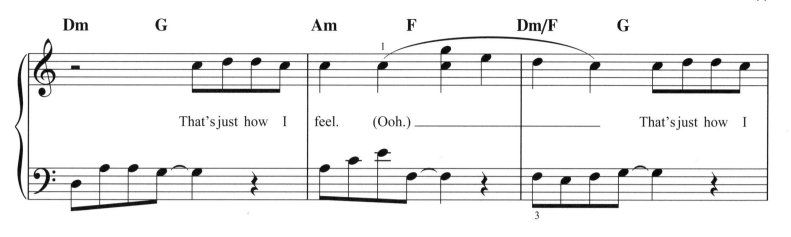

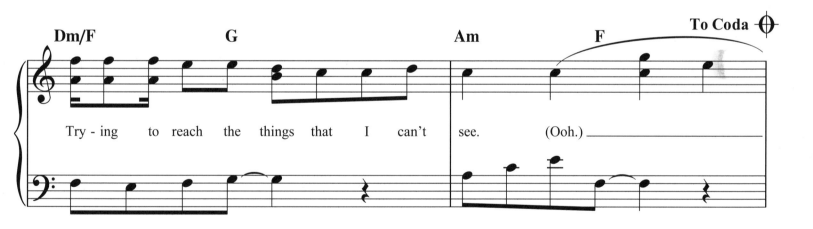

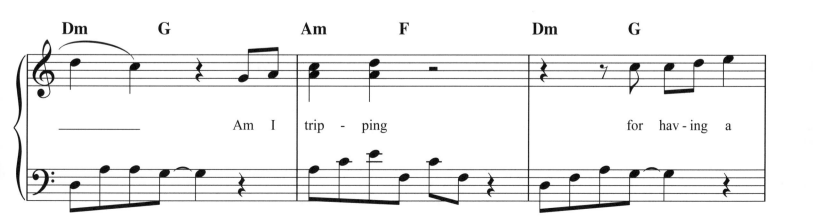

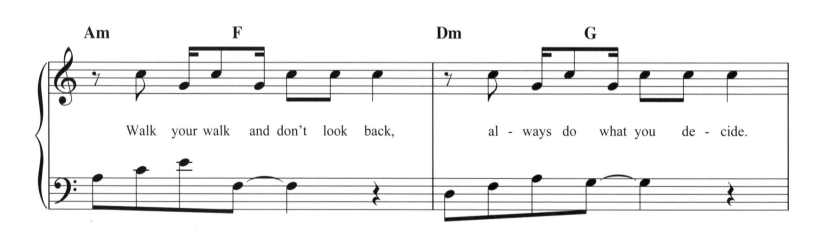

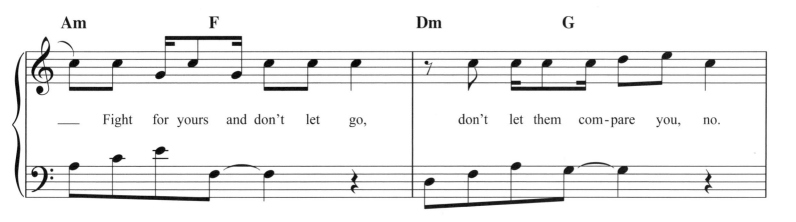

D.S. al Coda

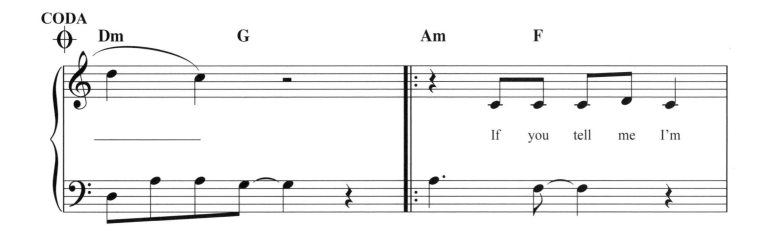

If you tell me I'm wrong, ____ wrong, ____ I don't wan - na be

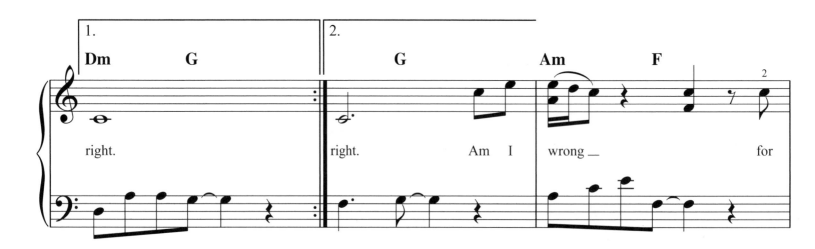

1.
right.

2.
right. Am I wrong ____ for

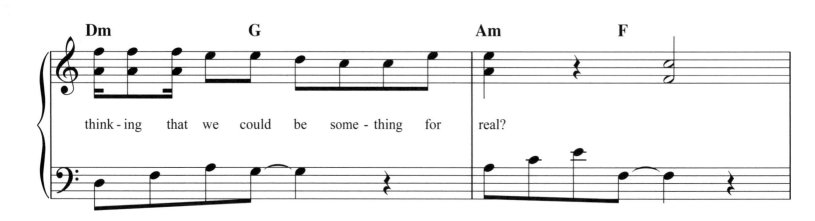

think - ing that we could be some - thing for real?

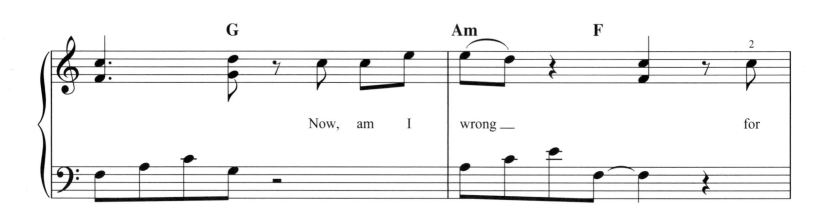

Now, am I wrong ____ for

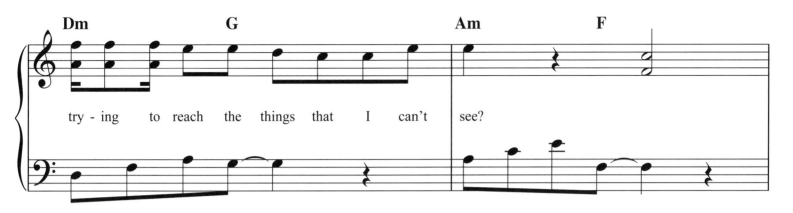

try-ing   to reach   the things   that   I   can't   see?

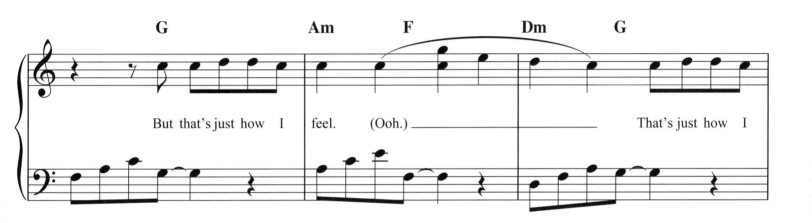

But that's just how   I   feel.   (Ooh.) _____   That's just how   I

feel. _____   That's just how   I   feel. _____
(Ooh.) _____

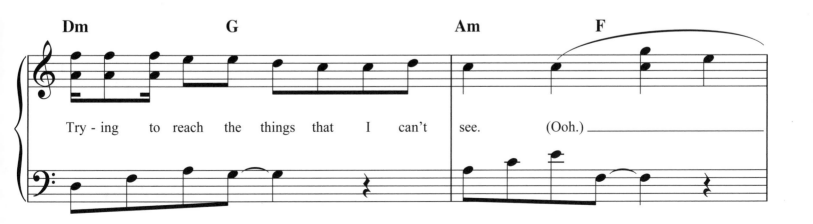

Try-ing   to reach   the things   that   I   can't   see.   (Ooh.) _____

So am I wrong ___ (Am I wrong?) for

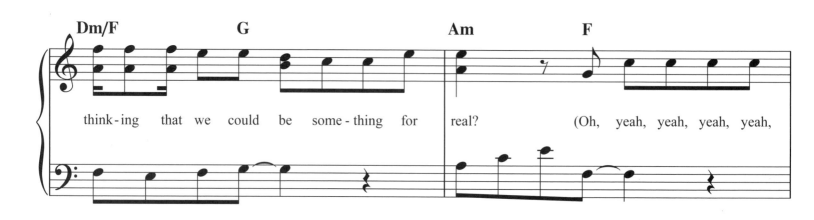

think-ing that we could be some-thing for real? (Oh, yeah, yeah, yeah, yeah,

oh.) ___ Now, am I wrong ___ (Am I wrong?) for

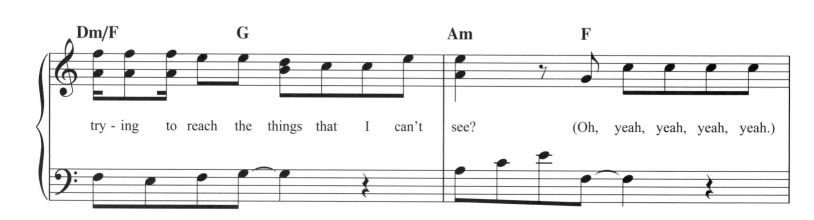

try-ing to reach the things that I can't see? (Oh, yeah, yeah, yeah, yeah.)

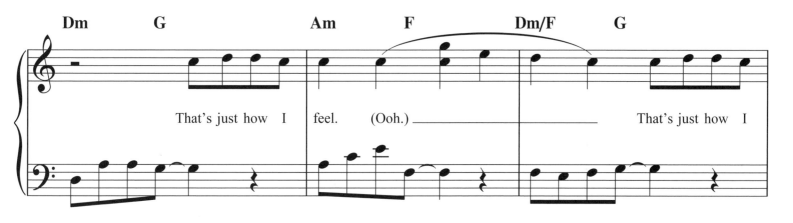

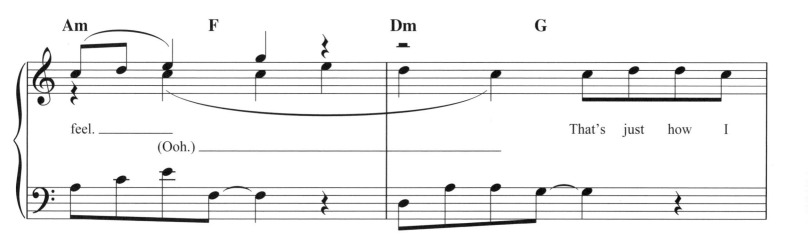

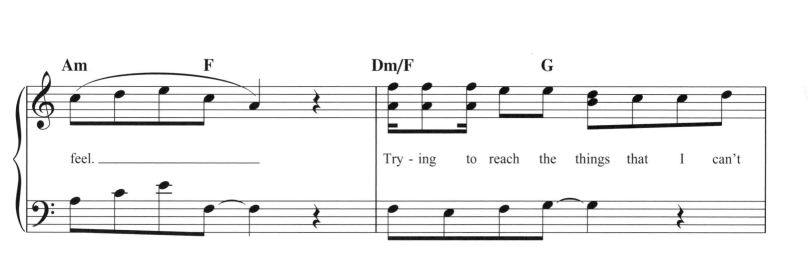

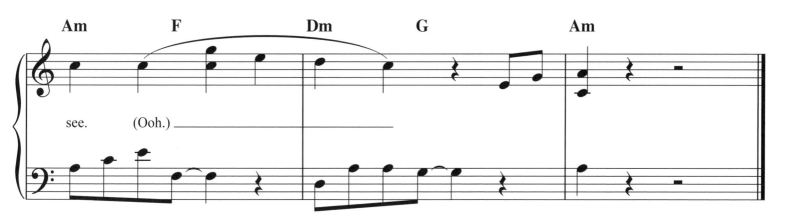

BEST DAY OF MY LIFE

Words and Music by ZACHARY BARNETT,
JAMES ADAM SHELLEY, MATTHEW SANCHEZ,
DAVID RUBLIN, SHEP GOODMAN
and AARON ACCETTA

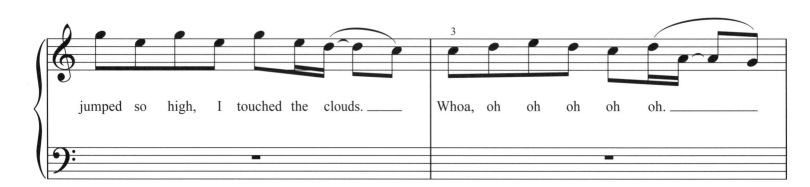

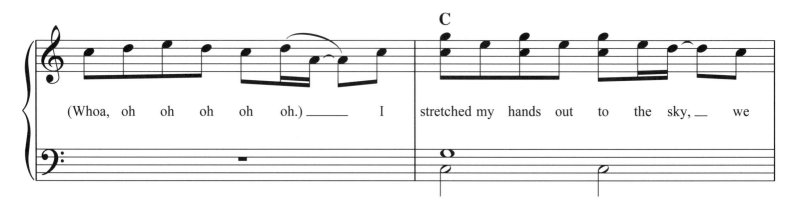

C

howled _ at the moon with friends _ and then the sun came crash - ing in. _____

F

Whoa, oh oh oh oh oh. _____ (Whoa, oh oh oh oh oh.) _____ But

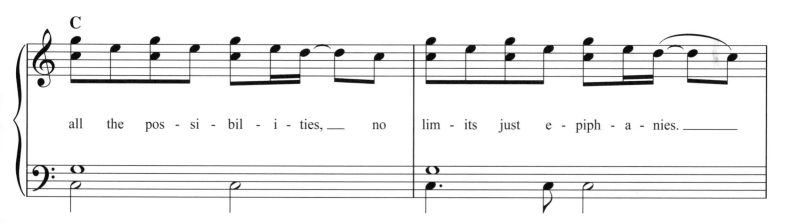

C

all the pos - si - bil - i - ties, _ no lim - its just e - piph - a - nies. _____

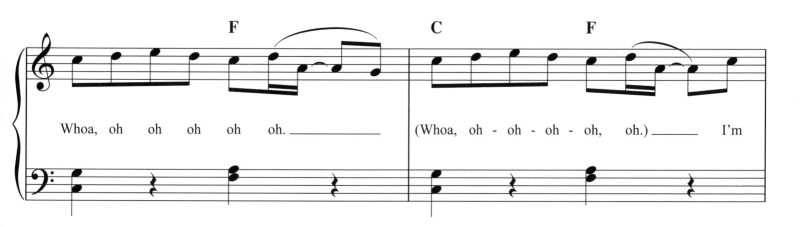

Whoa, oh oh oh oh oh. _____ **F** **C** (Whoa, oh - oh - oh - oh, oh.) _____ **F** I'm

never gon - na look back, whoa. ___ I'm nev - er gon - na give it up, no. _____

Just don't wake me now.

woo.

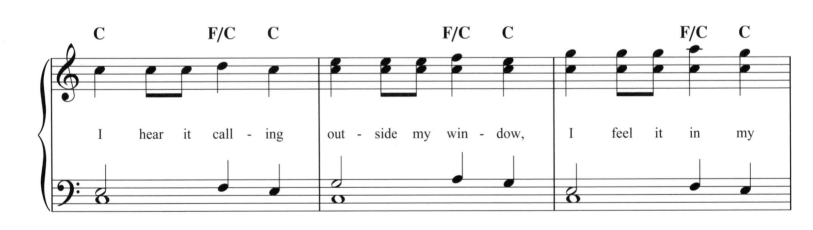

I hear it call - ing out - side my win - dow, I feel it in my

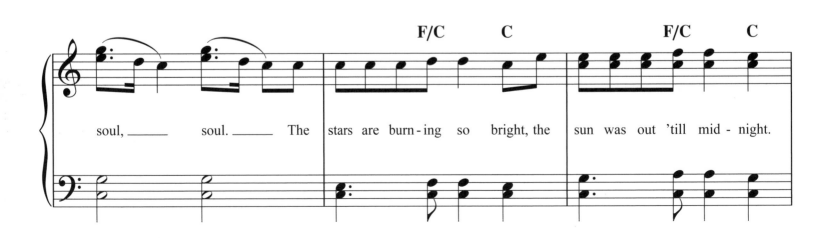

soul, _____ soul. _____ The stars are burn - ing so bright, the sun was out 'till mid - night.

I say we lose con - trol, _____ con - trol. _____

Woo, woo, _____ woo.

Woo, woo, _____ woo. This is gon-na be the best day of my life. _____ My

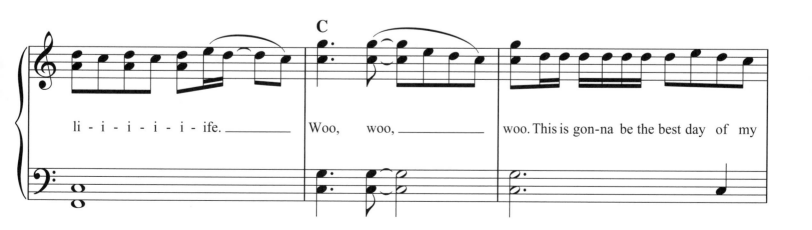

li - i - i - i - i - ife. _____ Woo, woo, _____ woo. This is gon-na be the best day of my

life. _____ My li - i - i - i - i - ife. _____ Woo, woo. _____

Ev - 'ry-thing is look-ing up, ev - 'ry-bod - y up now. Woo, woo. _____

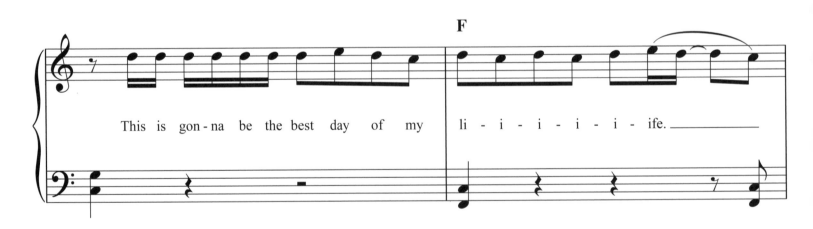

This is gon-na be the best day of my li - i - i - i - i - ife. _____

This is gon-na be the best day of my li - i - i - i - i - ife. _____

DARK HORSE

Words and Music by KATY PERRY,
JORDAN HOUSTON, LUKASZ GOTTWALD,
SARAH HUDSON, MAX MARTIN
and HENRY WALTER

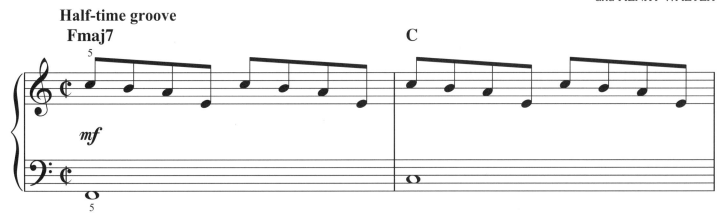

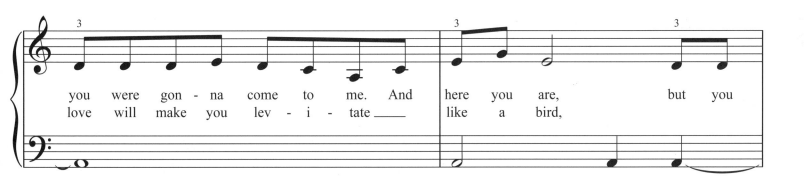

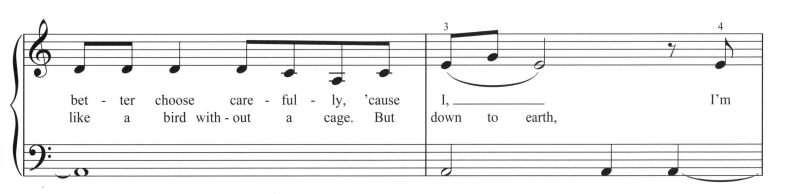

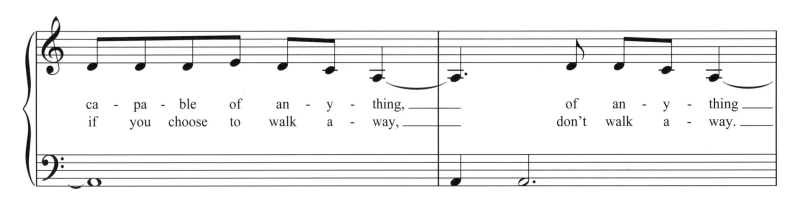

ca - pa - ble of an - y - thing, _____ of an - y - thing _____
if you choose to walk a - way, _____ don't walk a - way. _____

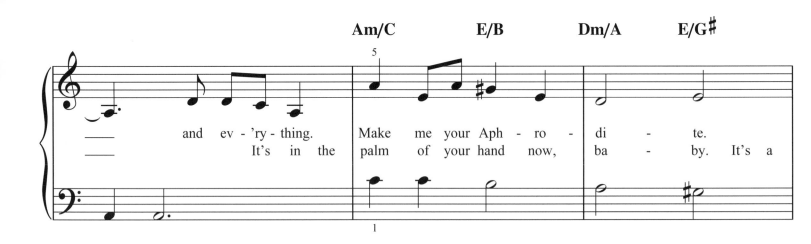

Am/C E/B Dm/A E/G♯

_____ and ev - 'ry - thing. Make me your Aph - ro - di - te.
_____ It's in the palm of your hand now, ba - by. It's a

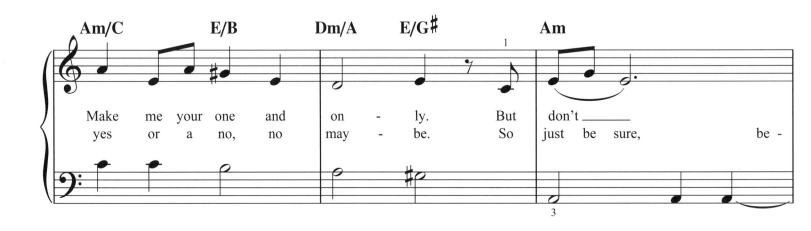

Am/C E/B Dm/A E/G♯ Am

Make me your one and on - ly. But don't _____
yes or a no, no may - be. So just be sure, be -

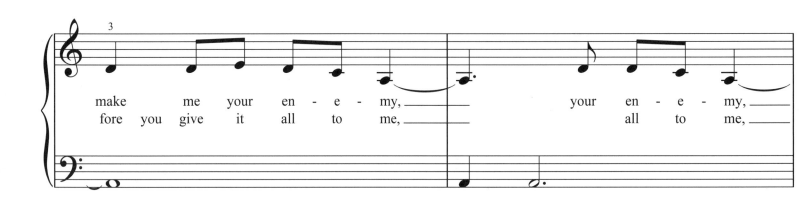

make me your en - e - my, _____ your en - e - my, _____
fore you give it all to me, _____ all to me, _____

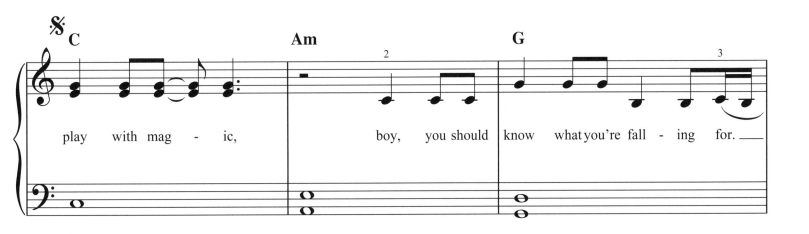

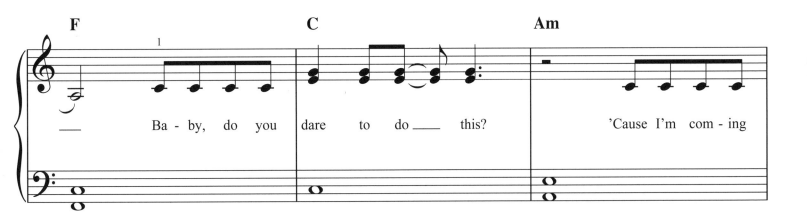

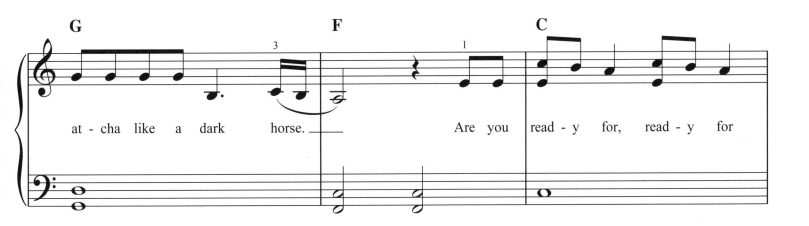

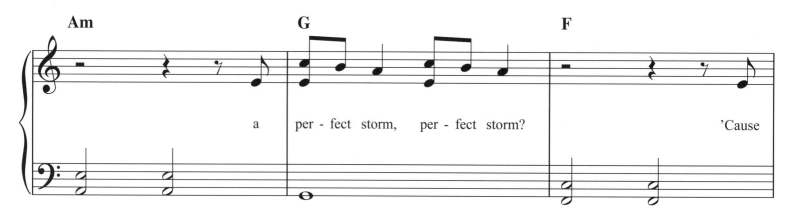

a per - fect storm, per - fect storm? 'Cause

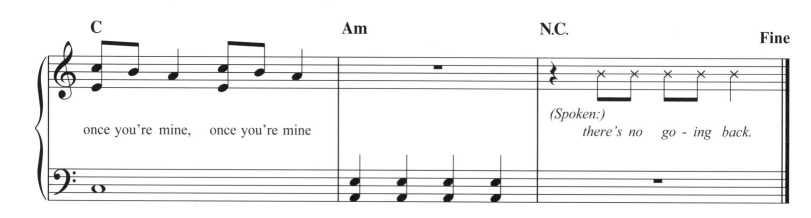

once you're mine, once you're mine

(Spoken:)
there's no go - ing back.

1.

(See rap lyrics)

2.

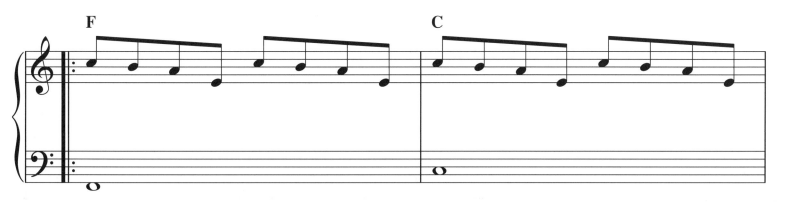

So, you want to

Rap lyrics

Uh, she's a beast, I call her Karma,
She'll eat your heart out like Jeffrey Dahmer.
Be careful, try not to lead her on.
Shorty heart is on steroids, 'cause her love is so strong.
You may fall in love when you meet her,
If you get the chance, you better keep her.
She's sweet as pie, but if you break her heart,
She'll turn cold as a freezer.
That fairy tale ending with a knight in shining armor,
She can be my Sleeping Beauty.
I'm gon' put her in a coma.
Now I think I love her,
Shorty so bad, sprung and I don't care
She ride me like a roller coaster,
Turned the bedroom into a fair.
Her love is like a drug,
I was tryna hit it and quit it,
But lil' mama so dope,
I messed around and got addicted.

FANCY

Words and Music by CHARLOTTE AITCHISON,
JONATHAN SHAVE, GEORGE ASTASIO,
JASON PEBWORTH, KURTIS McKENZIE,
JON TURNER and AMETHYST KELLY

from L. - A. to To - ky - o.   I'm so fan - cy,   can't you taste this gold? _ Re -

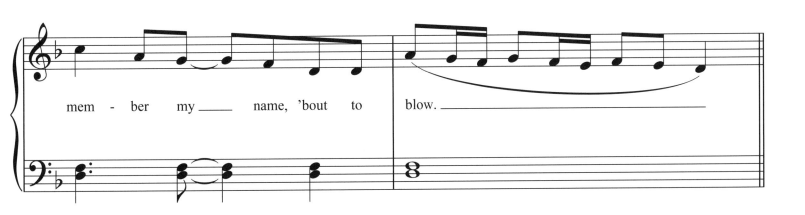

mem - ber my ____ name, 'bout to   blow. _____

N.C.

Rap 2: *(See additional lyrics)*
(Hey, hey, hey, hey,   hey, hey, hey, hey,   hey, hey, hey, hey,

hey, hey, hey, hey.)

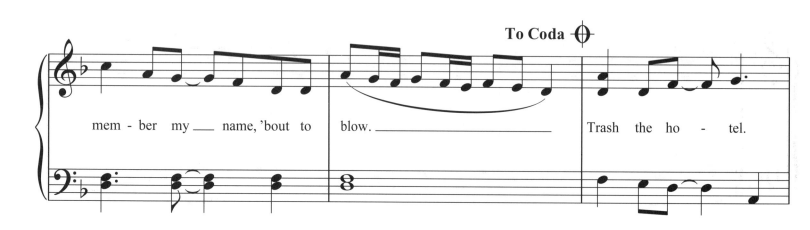

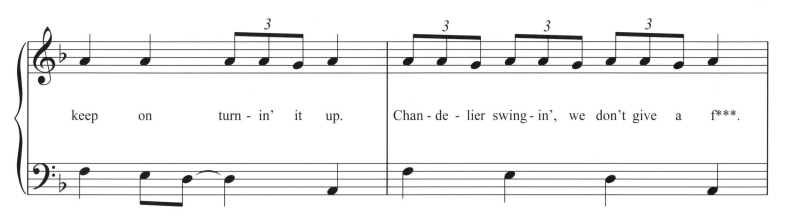
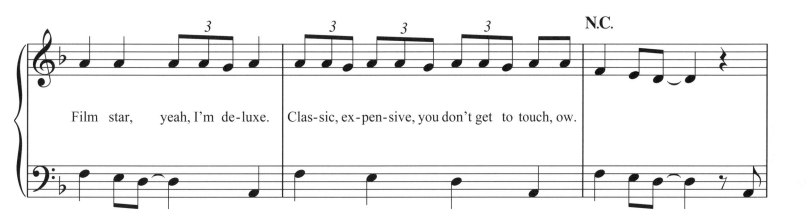

CODA

Additional Lyrics

Rap 1: First things first, I'm the realest. Drop this and let the whole world feel it. Let 'em feel it.
And I'm still in the Murda Bi'ness. I can hold you down like I'm givin' you lessons in physics.
Right, right.
You should want a bad bitch like this, hah? Drop it low and pick it up just like this, yeah.
Cup o' Ace, cup o' Goose, cup o' Cris. High heels, somethin' worth a half a ticket on my wrist,
On my wrist.
Takin' all the liquor straight, never chase that, never. Rooftop like we bringin' '88 back. What?
Bring the hooks in. Where the bass at? Champagne spillin', you should taste that.

Rap 2: I said, baby, I do this. I thought that you knew this. Can't stand no haters, and honest, the truth is.
And my flow retarded. HPD departed. Swagger on suit but I can't shop in no department
And get my money on time. If they got money, decline. And swear I'm in that there so much, better
give that line a rewind.
So get my money on time. If they got money, decline. I just can't worry 'bout no haters, gotta stay
on my grind.
Now tell me, who dat, who dat, dat do dat, do dat? Put that paper over all, I thought you knew dat,
knew dat.
I be the I-G-G-Y, put my name in bold. I been workin', I'm up in here with some change to throw.

Rap 3: Still stunting, how you love dat? Got the whole world askin' how I does that.
Hot girls, hands off. Don't touch that. Look at it, I bet you wishin' you could clutch that.
It's just the way you like it, huh? You're so good, he just wish-in' he could bite it, huh?
Never turn down money. Slayin' these hoes, gold trigger on the gun like...

LET IT GO

from Disney's Animated Feature FROZEN

Music and Lyrics by KRISTEN ANDERSON-LOPEZ
and ROBERT LOPEZ

Half-time feel, mysterious

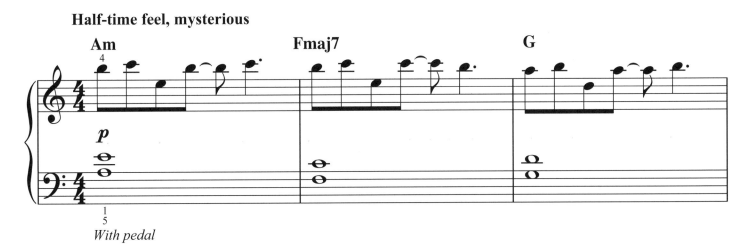

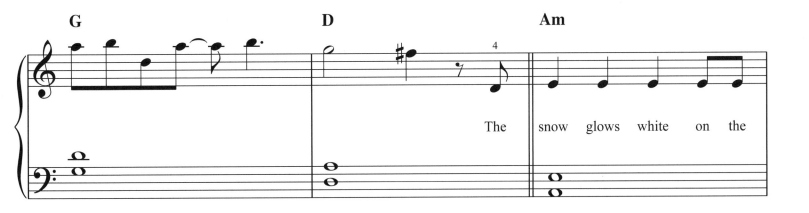

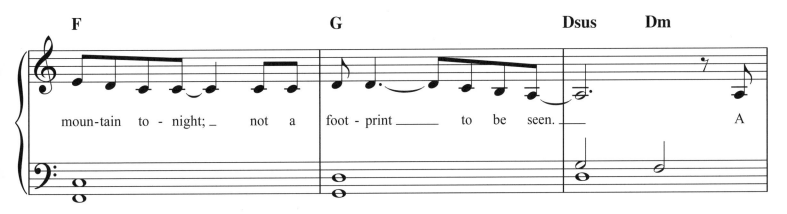

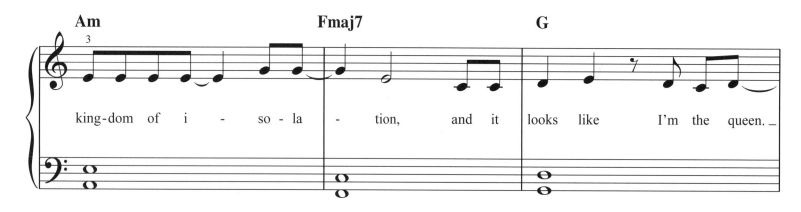

Am

Fmaj7

G

king-dom of i - so - la - tion, and it looks like I'm the queen.

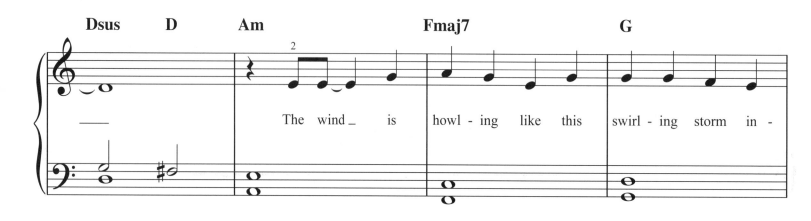

Dsus   **D**   **Am**

Fmaj7

G

The wind _ is howl - ing like this swirl - ing storm in -

Dm

Am

G

side. _____ Could - n't keep it in, _____ heav - en knows I _____

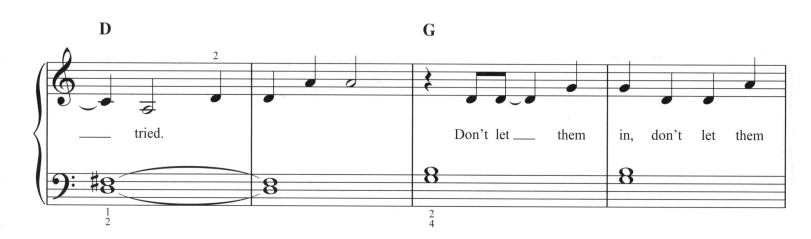

D

G

_____ tried. Don't let _____ them in, don't let them

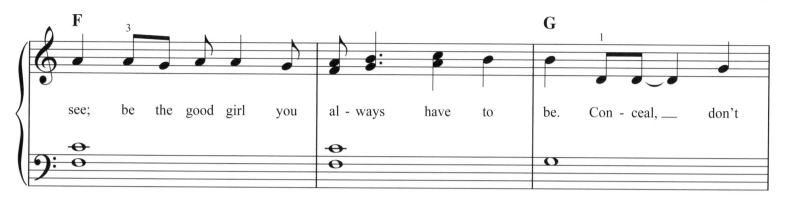

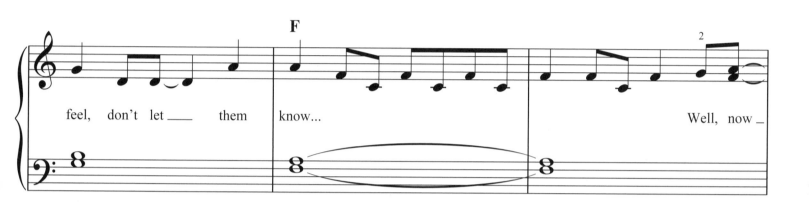

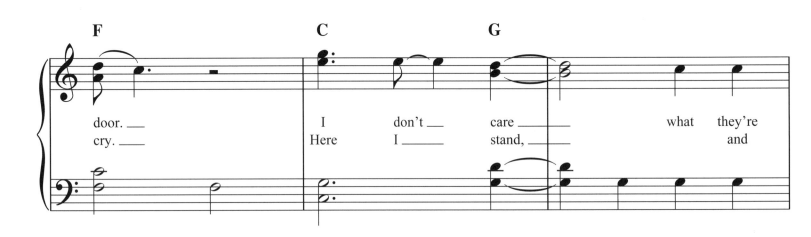

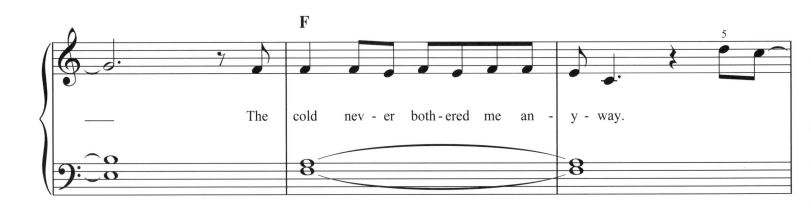

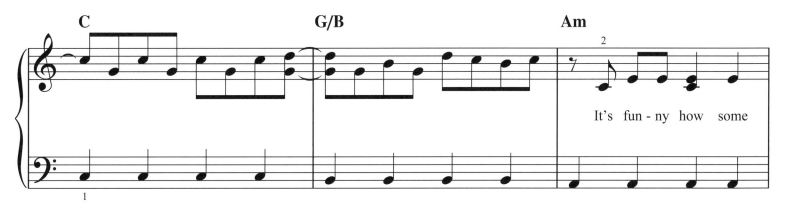

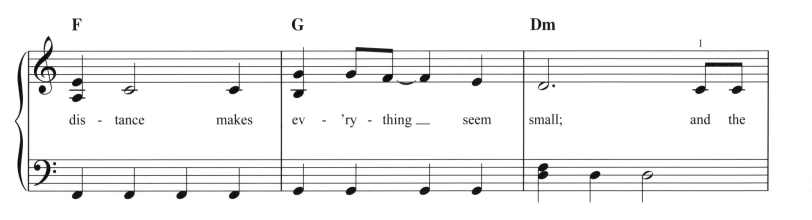

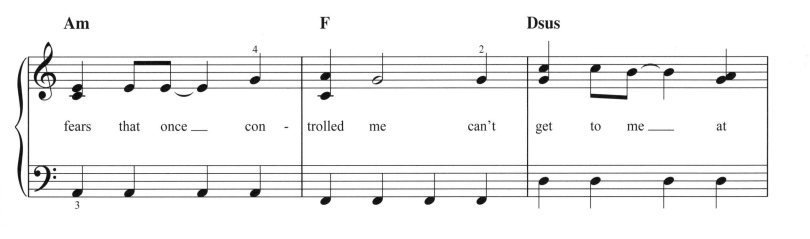

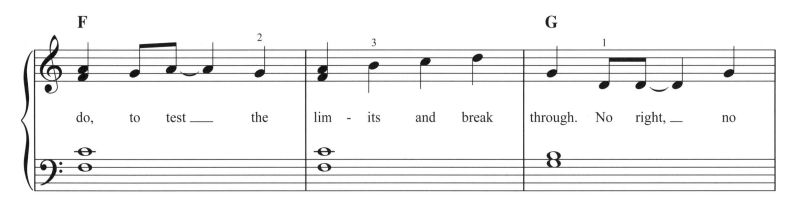

do, to test ___ the lim - its and break through. No right, ___ no

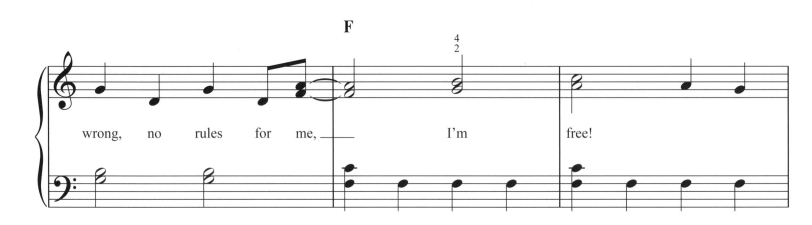

wrong, no rules for me, ___ I'm free!

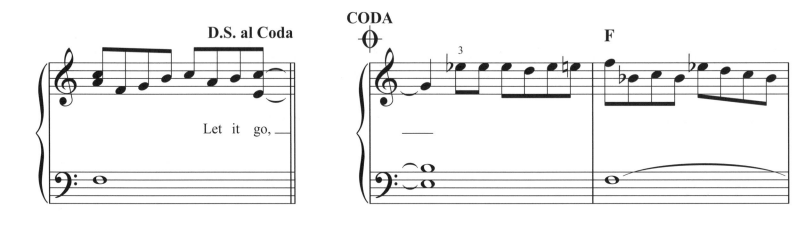

D.S. al Coda

Let it go, ___

CODA

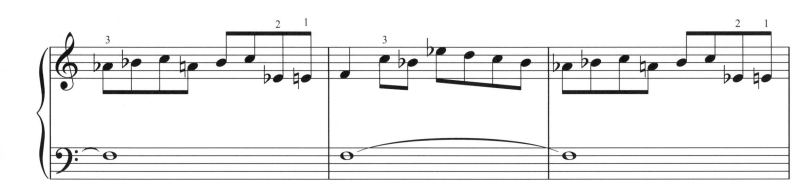

My pow - er flur - ries through the air in - to the

ground. My soul __ is spi - ral - ing in

G

fro - zen frac - tals all a - round. __ And one __ thought

cry - stal - li - zes like an i - cy blast:

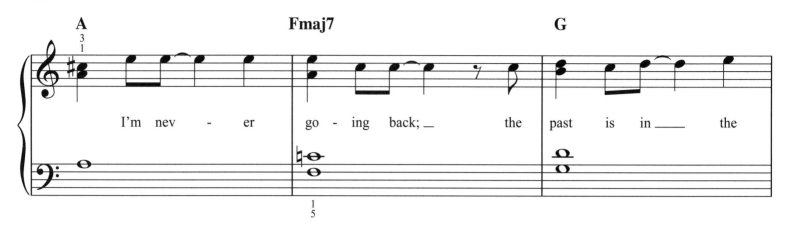

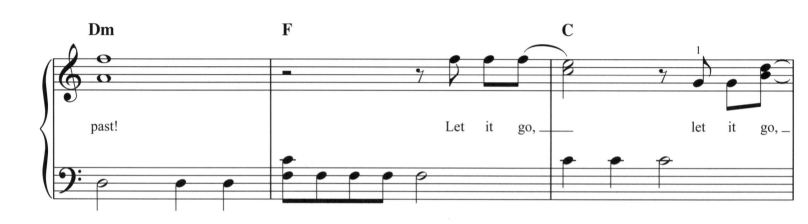

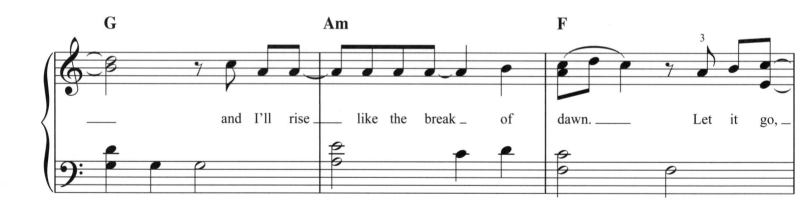

43

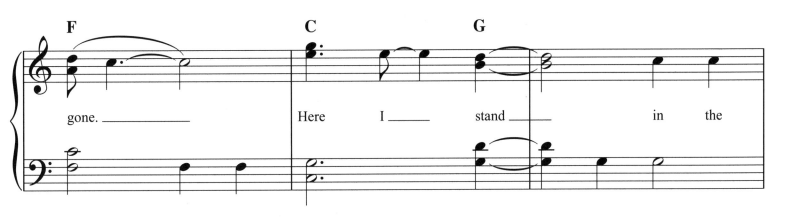

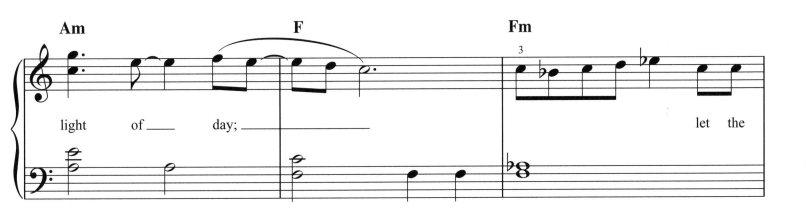

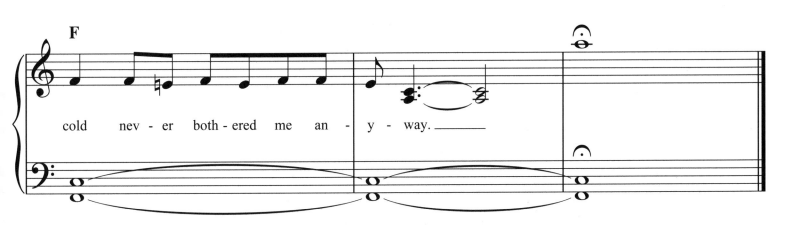

HAPPY
from DESPICABLE ME 2

Words and Music by
PHARRELL WILLIAMS

Moderately fast

I'm a hot air bal - loon ____ that could go to space
I should prob - 'bly warn ____ you, I'll be just ____ fine.

with the air like I don't
No of - fense to

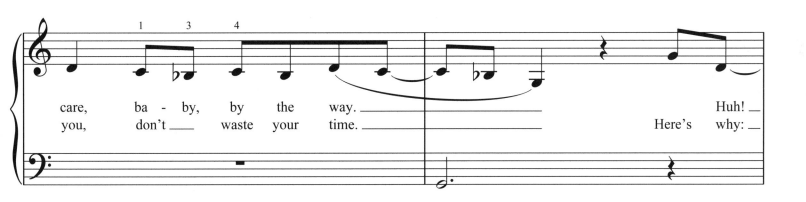

care, ba - by, by the way. ____ Huh! ____
you, don't ____ waste your time. ____ Here's why: ____

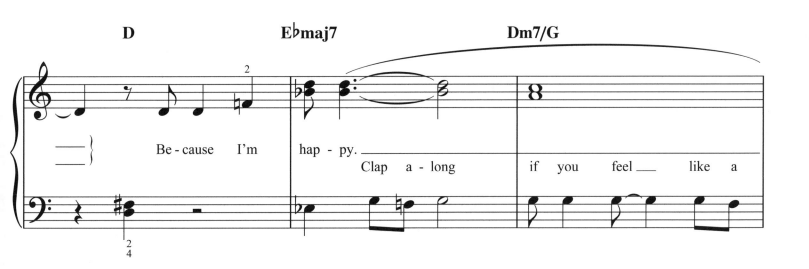

D   E♭maj7   Dm7/G

Be - cause I'm hap - py.
Clap a - long if you feel ____ like a

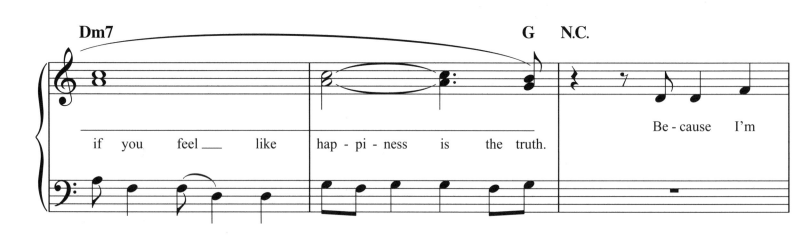

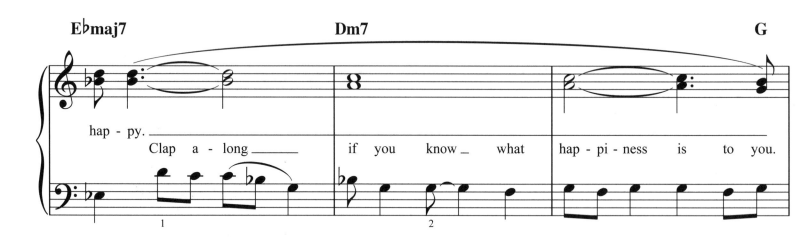

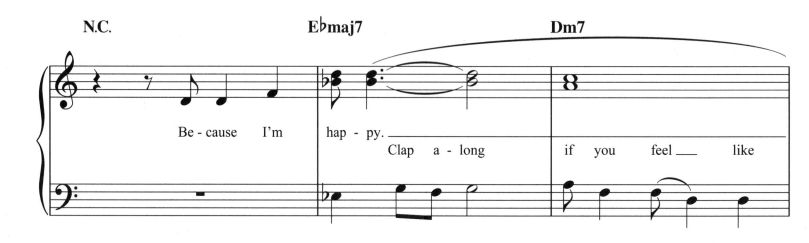

that's what you wan - na do.

Bring me down, ___

___ can't noth - in' bring me down; ___ your love is too

high. Bring me down, ___ can't noth - in' bring me down. ___

___ (Let me tell you now.) Bring me down, ___ can't noth - in'

bring me down; ___ your love is too high. Bring me down, __

___ can't noth - in' bring me down. ___ (Be - cause I'm

E♭maj7   Dm7/G   G

hap - py. ___
Clap a - long if you feel ___ like a room with - out a roof.

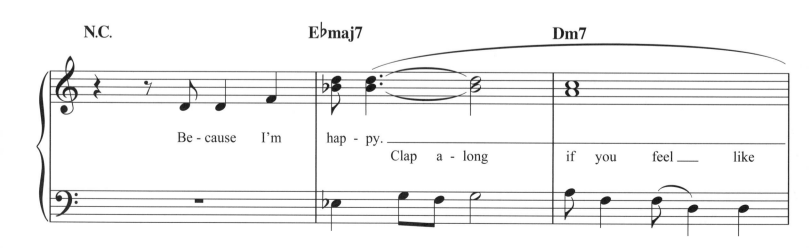

N.C.   E♭maj7   Dm7

Be - cause I'm hap - py. ___
Clap a - long if you feel ___ like

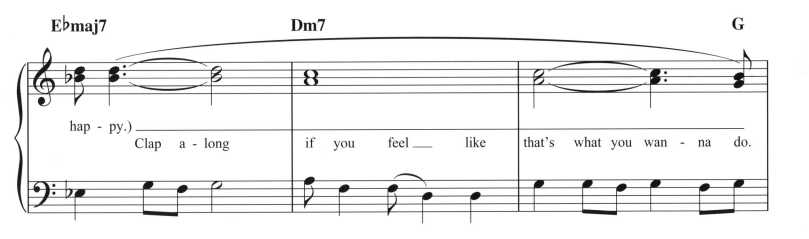

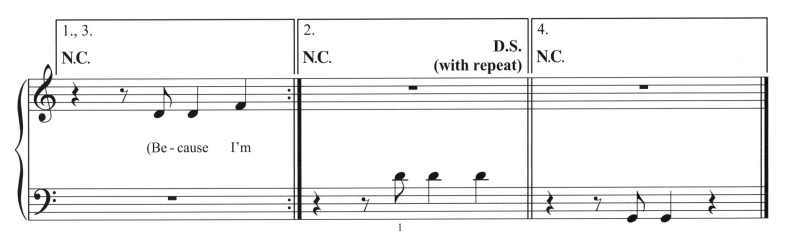

LOVE NEVER FELT SO GOOD

Words and Music by MICHAEL JACKSON
and PAUL ANKA

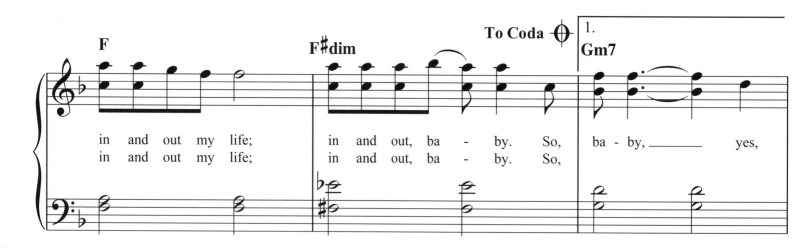

2.

Gm7   Gm7/C   F   Bb/C   D.S. al Coda

ba - by, _____ love nev - er felt so good.

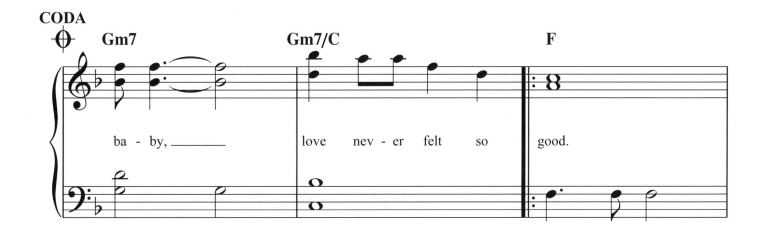

CODA

Gm7   Gm7/C   F

ba - by, _____ love nev - er felt so good.

C7sus   F   **1.** C7sus

It nev - er felt so ___ good. So, no, it nev - er felt so

2.

C7sus   F

no, it nev - er felt _____ so good.

rit.

LOVE SOMEONE

Words and Music by JASON MRAZ,
BECKY GEBHARDT, CHASKA POTTER,
MAI BLOOMFIELD, MONA TAVAKOLI,
CHRIS KEUP and STEWART MYERS

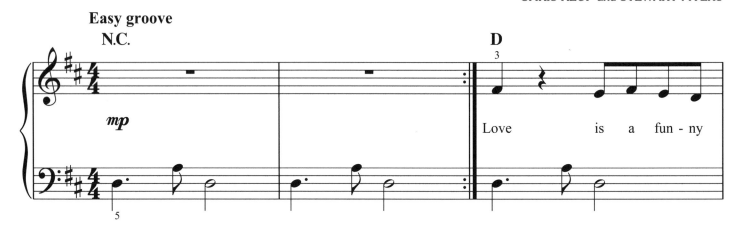

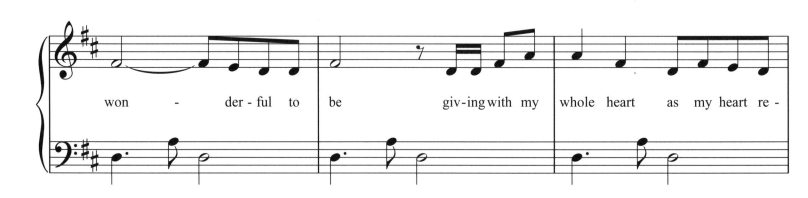

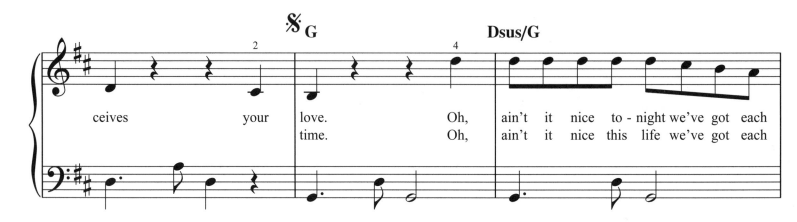

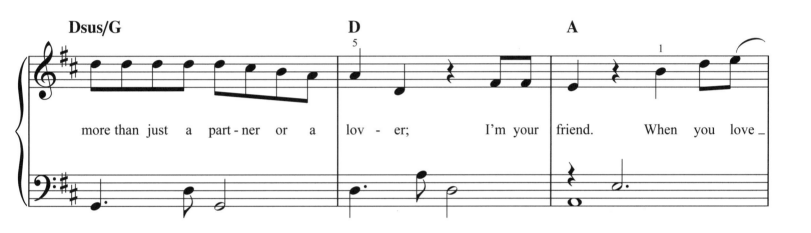

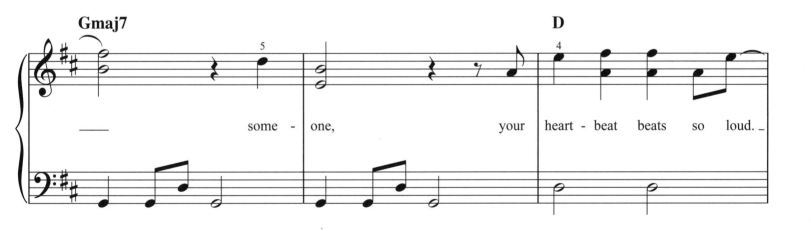

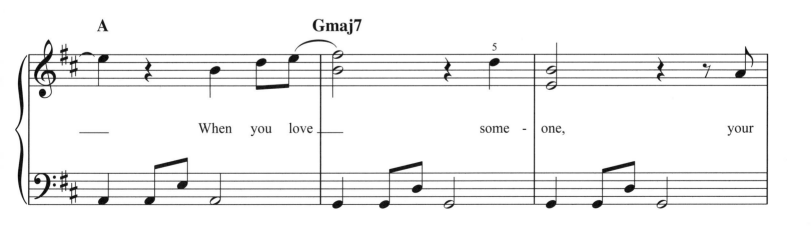

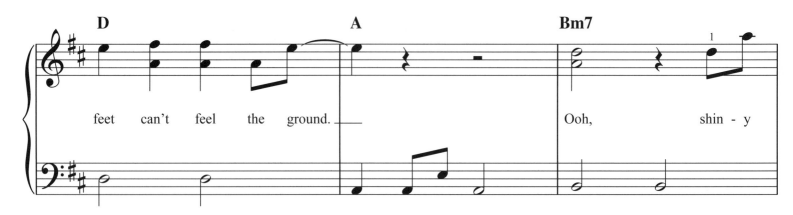

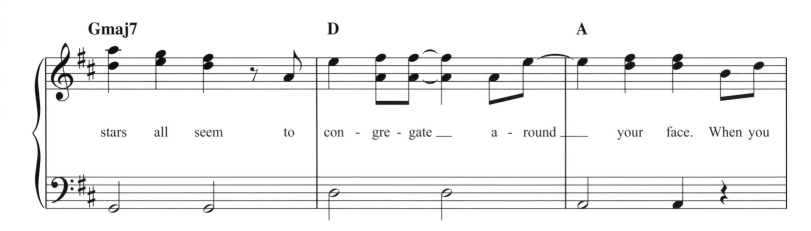

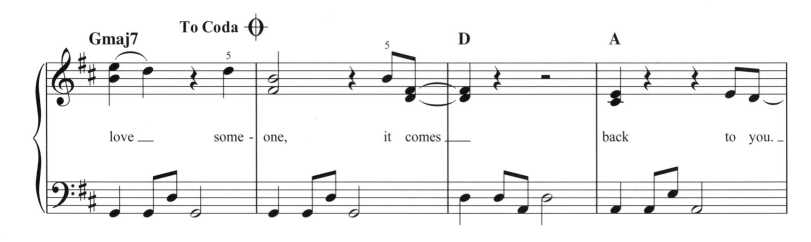

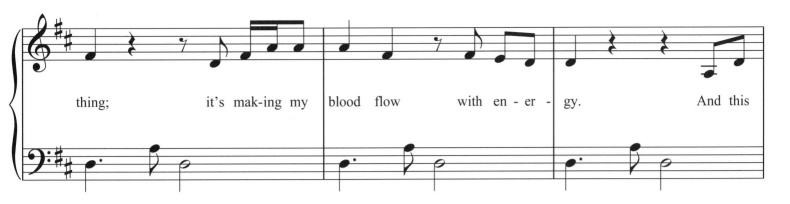

thing;   it's mak-ing my   blood flow   with en - er - gy.   And this

life,   an a - wak-ing dream,   is what I've been wish - ing   for is hap-pen-

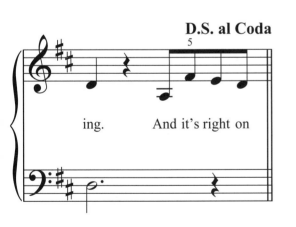

ing.   And it's right on

one,   when you love   some-

one.   We're gon - na give our-selves to   love to - night,

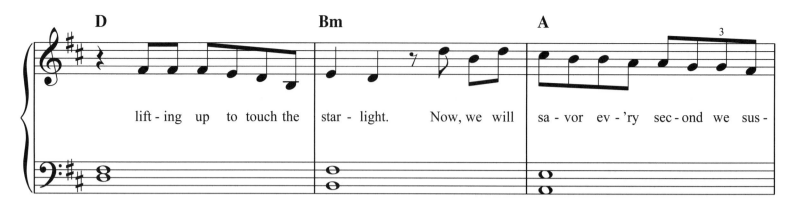

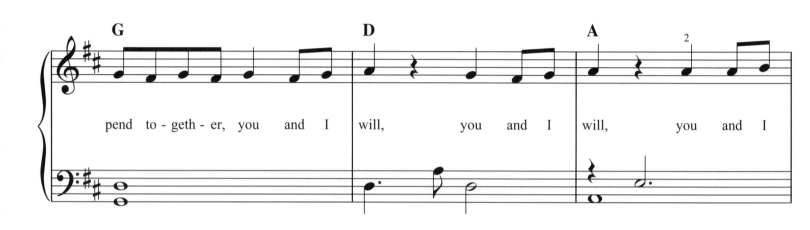

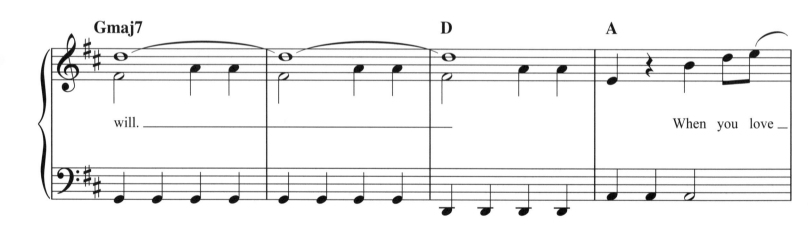

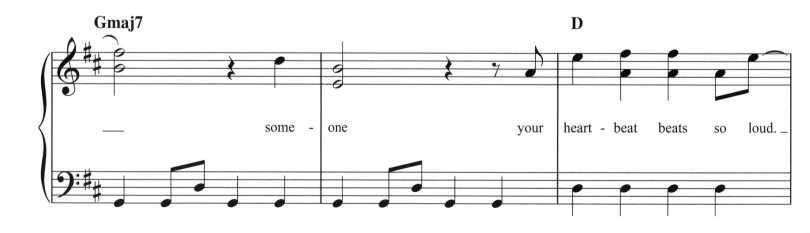

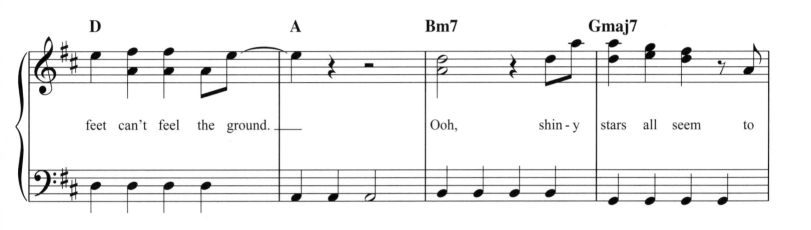

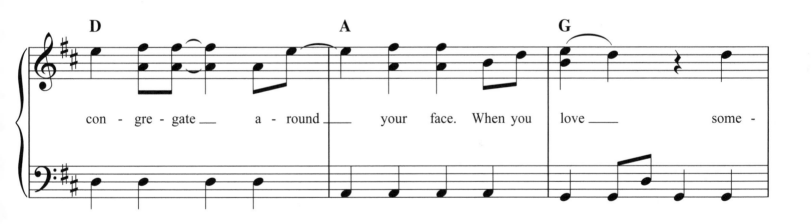

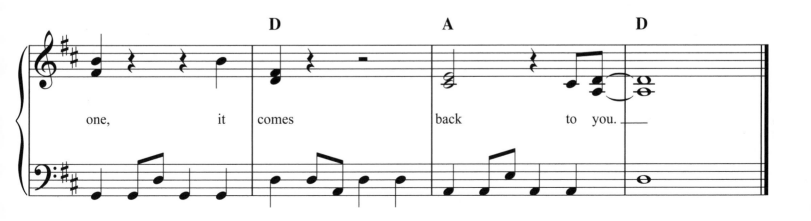

POMPEII

Words and Music by
DAN SMITH

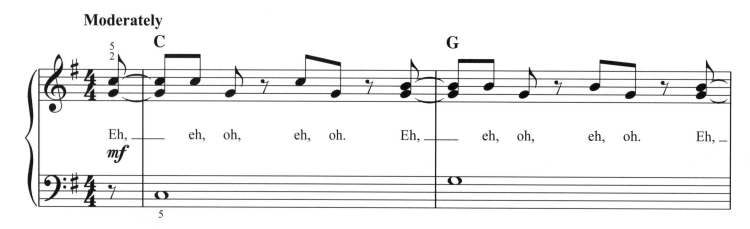

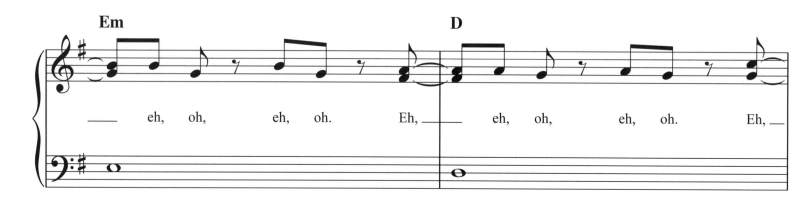

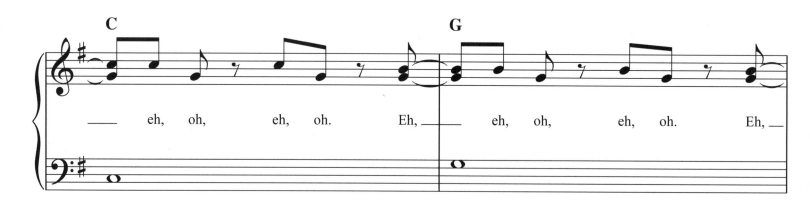

I was left to my own _____ de - vic - es.
We were caught up and lost _____ in all _____ of our

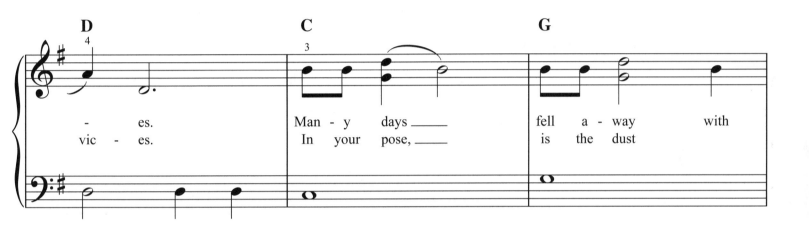

- es.
vic - es.

Man - y days _____
In your pose, _____

fell a - way with
is the dust

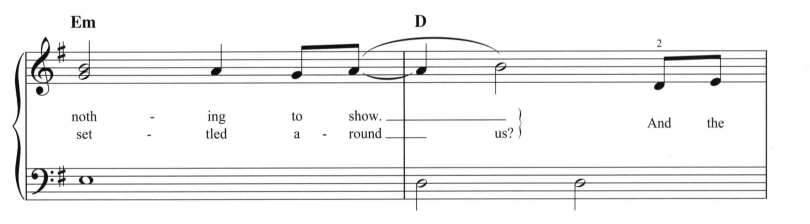

noth - ing to show. _____
set - tled a - round _____ us?

And the

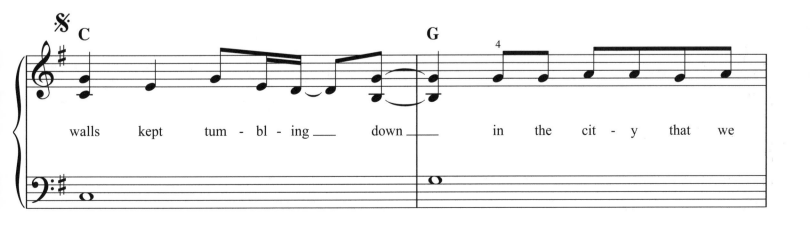

walls kept tum - bl - ing _____ down _____ in the cit - y that we

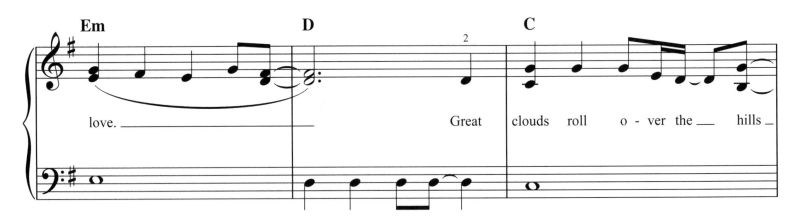

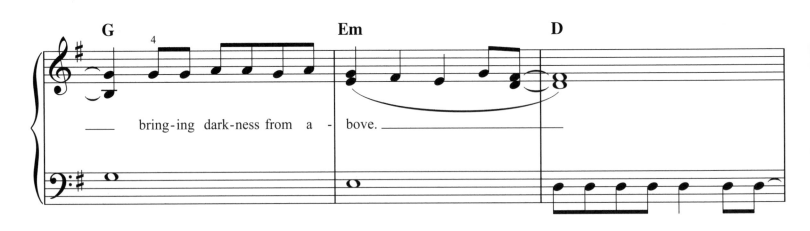

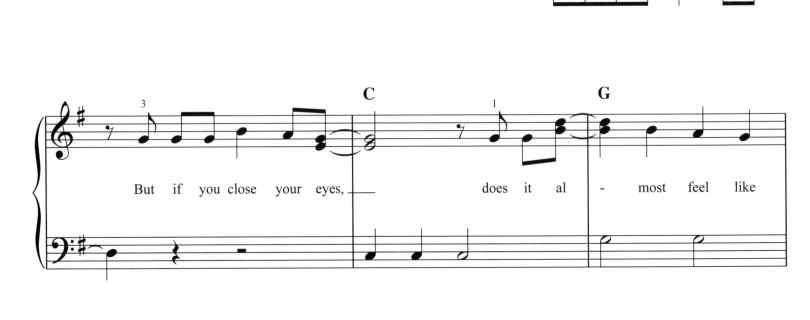

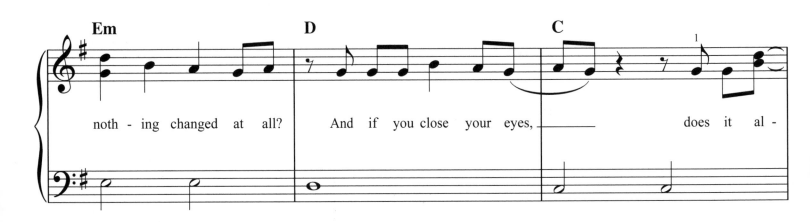

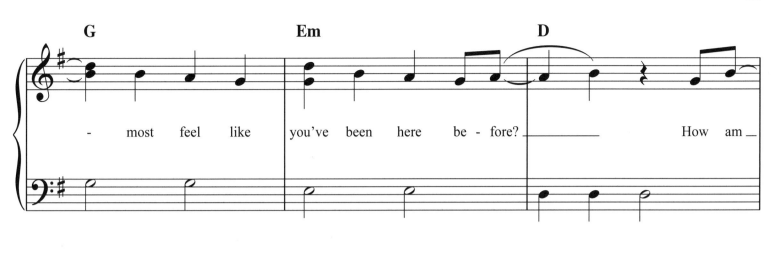

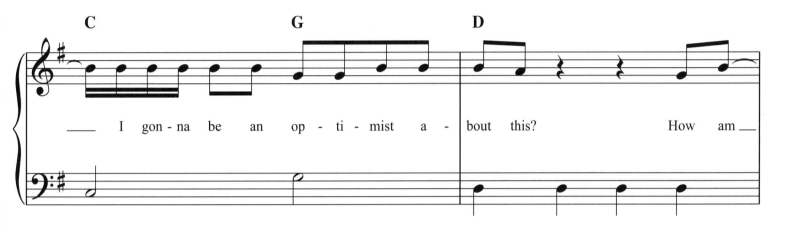

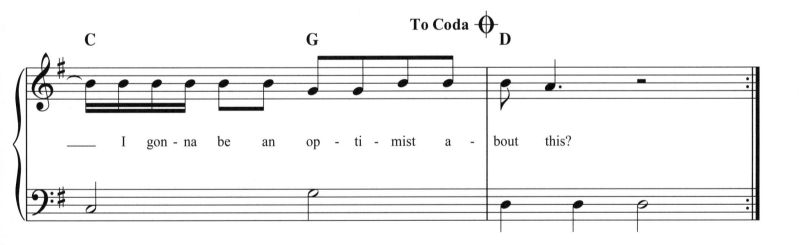

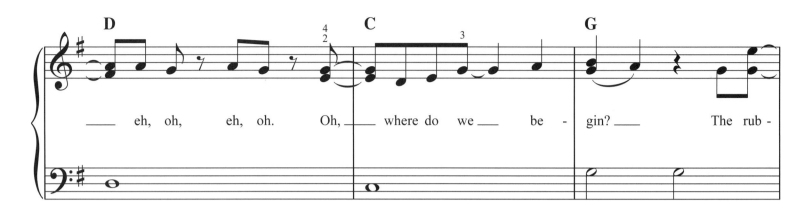

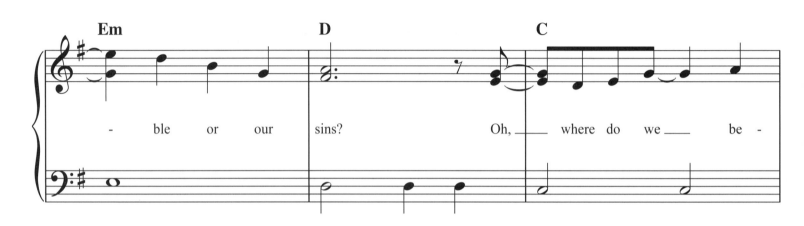

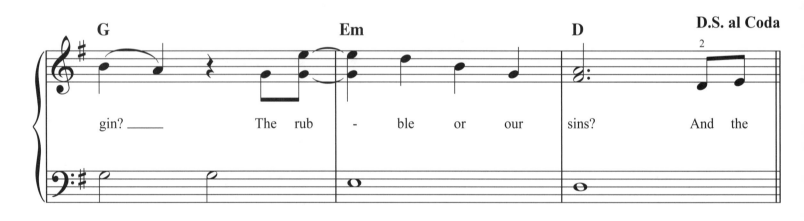

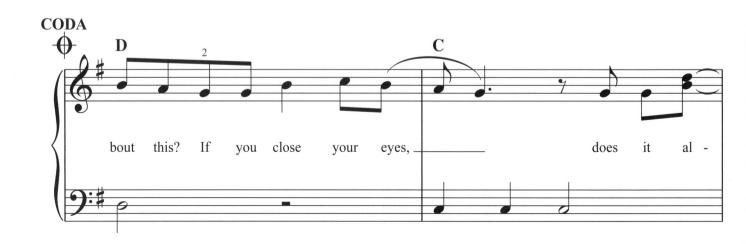

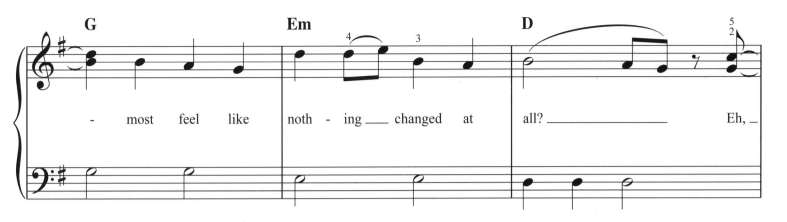

-most feel like noth - ing ___ changed at all? _____ Eh, __

___ eh, oh, eh, oh. Eh, ___ eh, oh, eh, oh. Eh, __

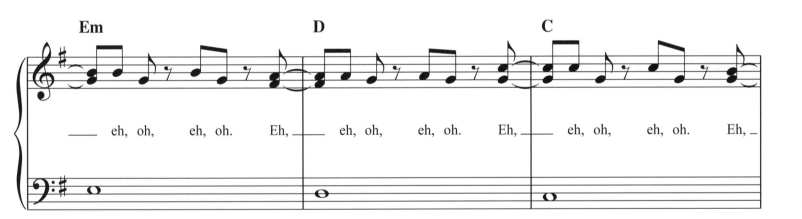

___ eh, oh, eh, oh. Eh, ___ eh, oh, eh, oh. Eh, ___ eh, oh, eh, oh. Eh, __

___ eh, oh, eh, oh. Eh, ___ eh, oh, eh, oh. Eh, ___ eh, oh, eh, oh.

PROBLEM

Words and Music by ILYA,
ARIANA GRANDE, MAX MARTIN,
SAVAN KOTECHA and AMETHYST AMELIA KELLY

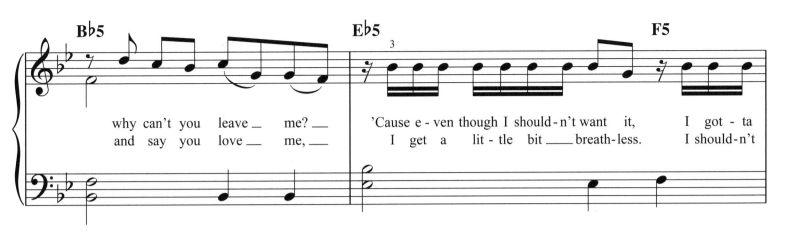

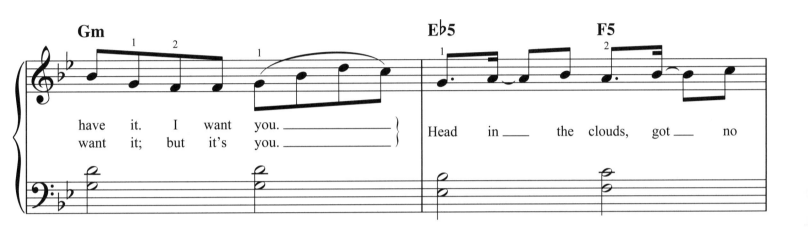

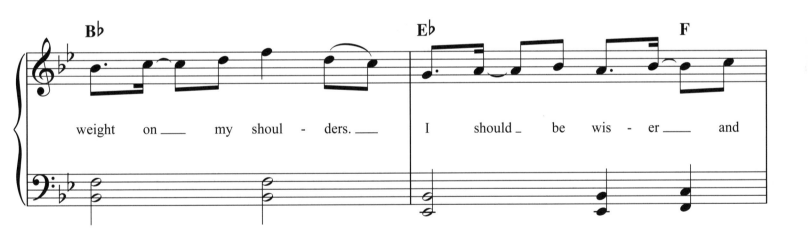

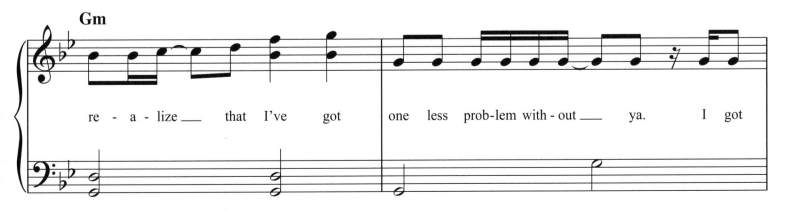

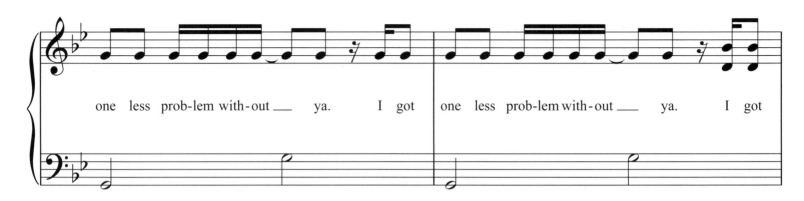

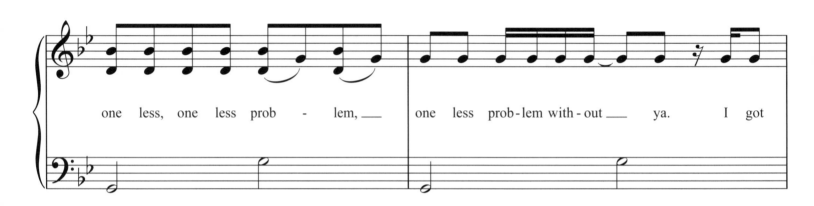

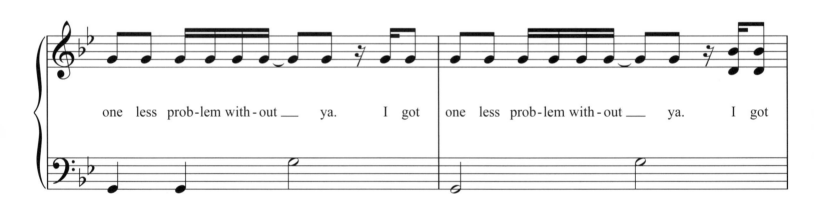

Rap: *(See additional lyrics)*

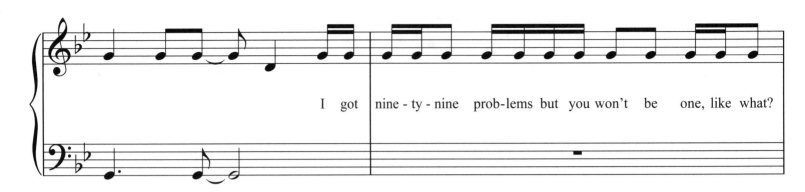

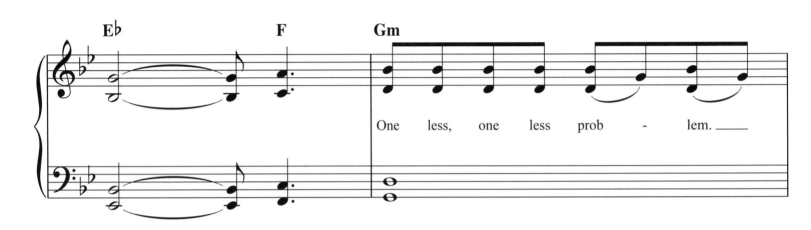

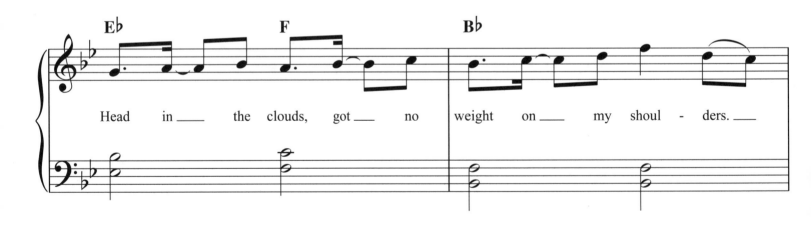

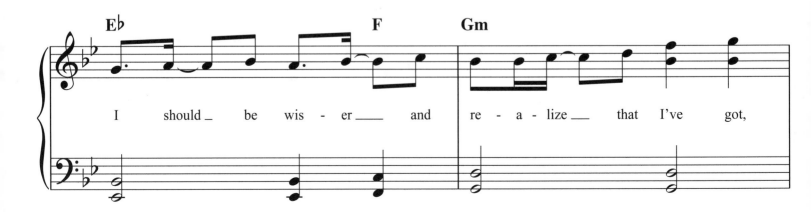

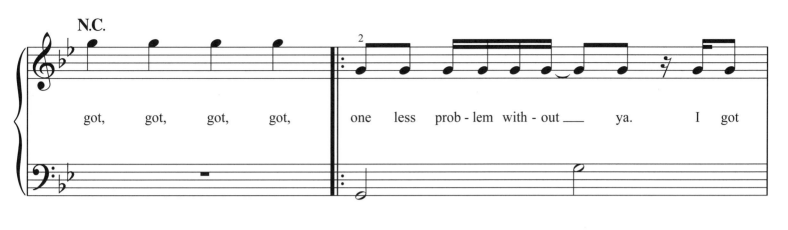

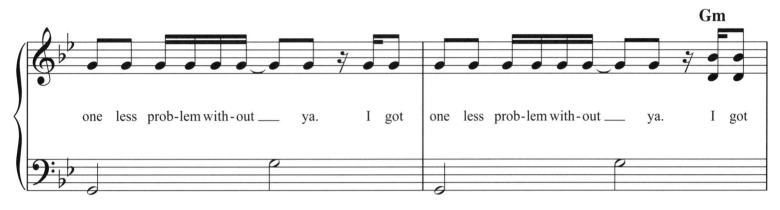

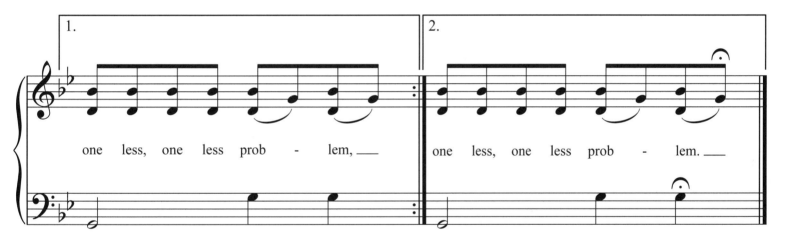

Additional Lyrics

Rap: Smart money bettin' I'll be better off without you.
In no time I'll be forgettin' all about you.
You sayin' that you know, but I really, really doubt.
You understand? My life is easy when I ain't around you.
Iggy, Iggy too biggie to be here stressin'.
I'm thinkin' I love the thought of you more than I love your presence.
And the best thing now is probably for you to exit.
I let you go, let you back. I finally learned my lesson.
No half-steppin', either you want it or you just playin'.
I'm listenin' to you knowin' I can't believe what you're sayin'.
There's a million you's, baby boo, so don't be dumb.
(I got 99 problems but you won't be one, like what?)

RAGING FIRE

Words and Music by PHILLIP PHILLIPS,
GREGG WATTENBERG, DEREK FUHRMANN
and TODD CLARK

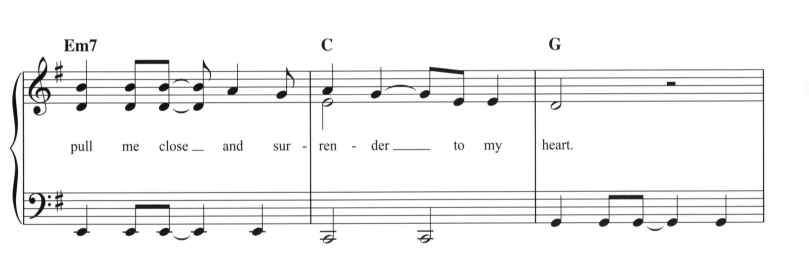

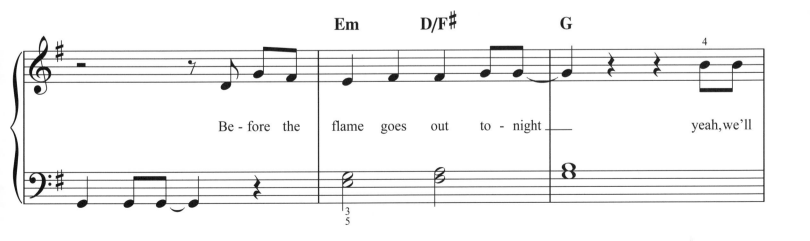

74

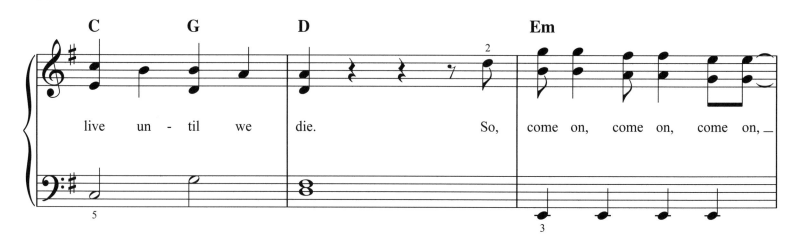

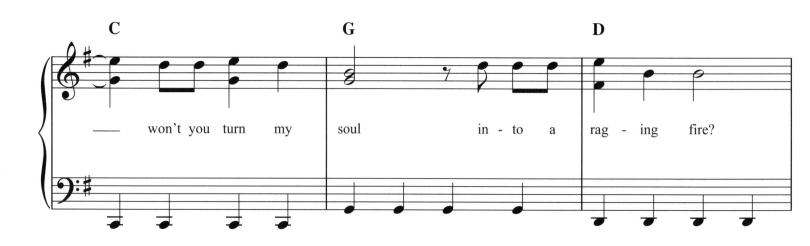

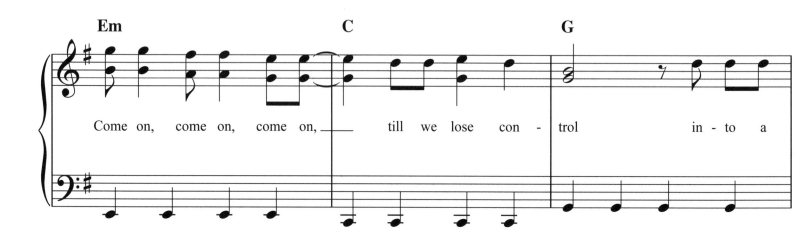

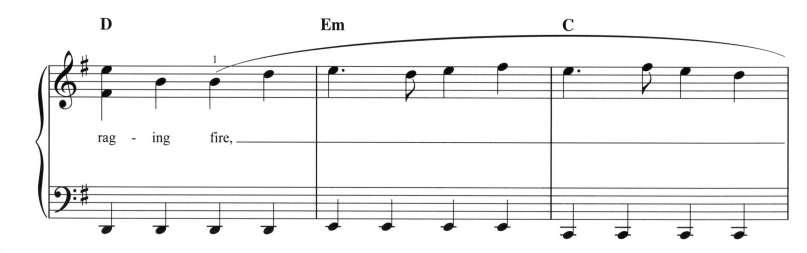

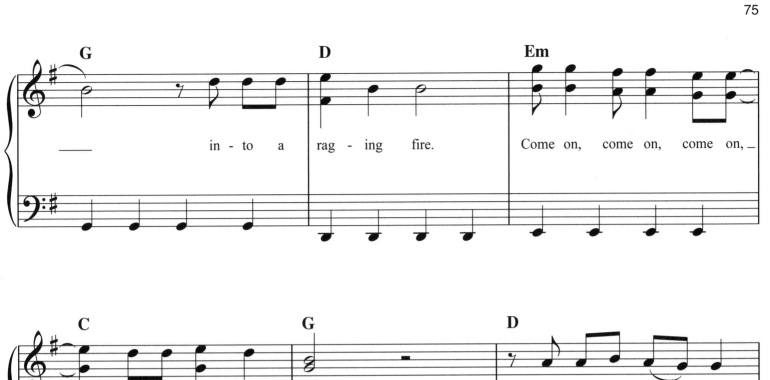

into a rag - ing fire. Come on, come on, come on, ___

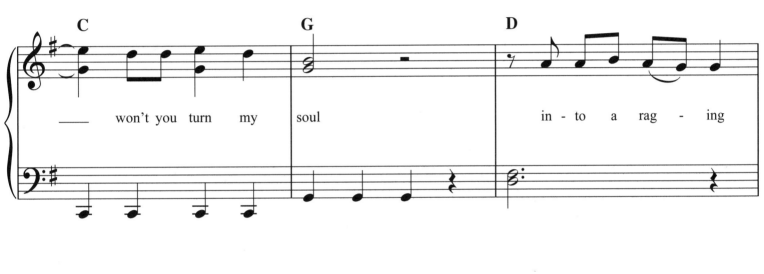

___ won't you turn my soul into a rag - ing

fire?

You know time will give ___ and time will take. All the

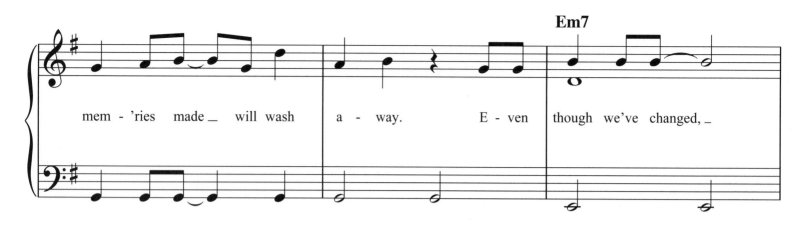

mem - 'ries made _ will wash a - way. E - ven though we've changed, _

I'm still here with you. If you lis - ten close, you'll

hear the sound of all the ghosts that bring us down. _____

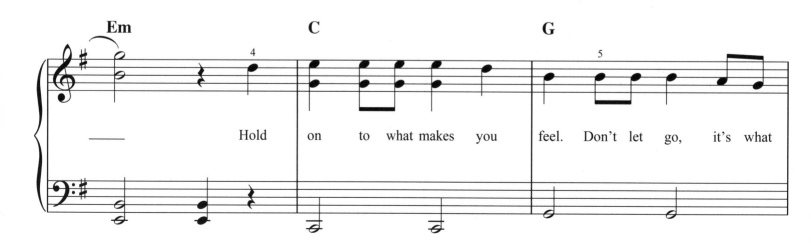

_____ Hold on to what makes you feel. Don't let go, it's what

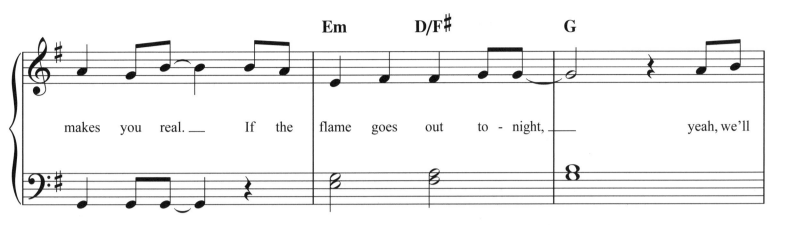

makes you real. ___ If the flame goes out to-night, ___ yeah, we'll

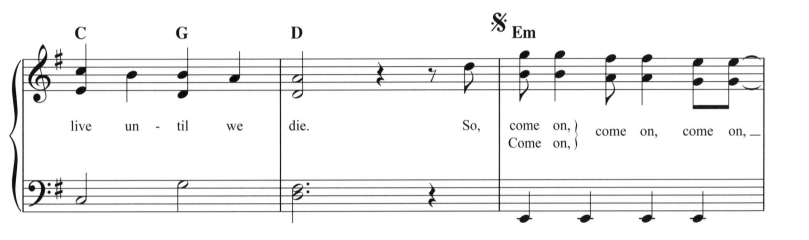

live un - til we die. So, come on, come on, come on, ___
Come on,

___ won't you turn my soul in - to a rag - ing fire?

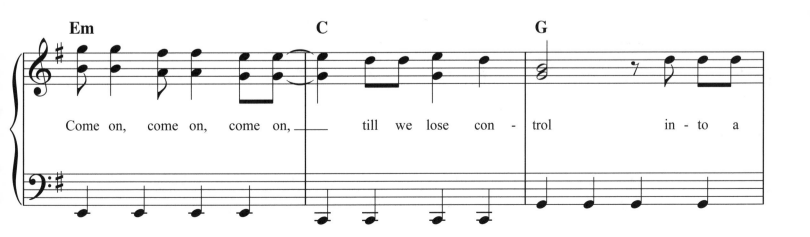

Come on, come on, come on, ___ till we lose con - trol in - to a

rag - ing fire, _____

in - to a rag - ing fire. Come on, come on, come on, _____

_____ won't you turn my soul   in - to a rag - ing

fire?

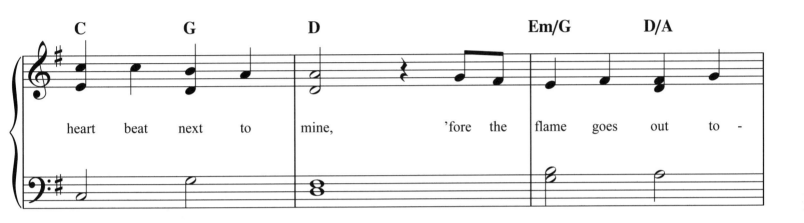

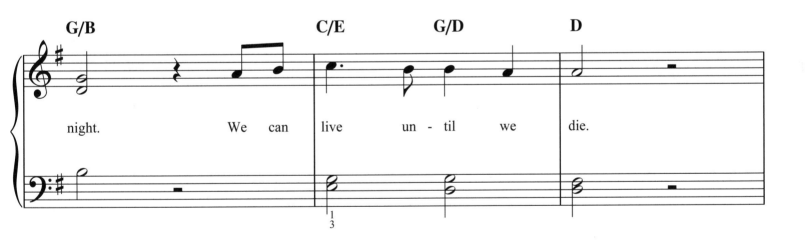

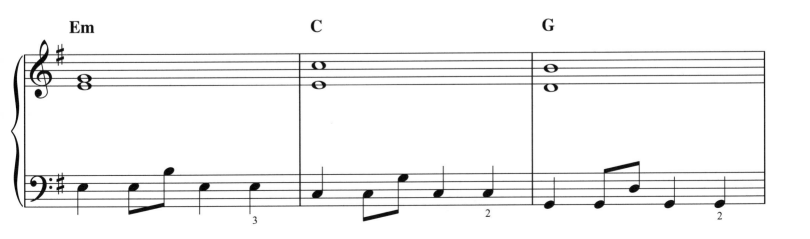

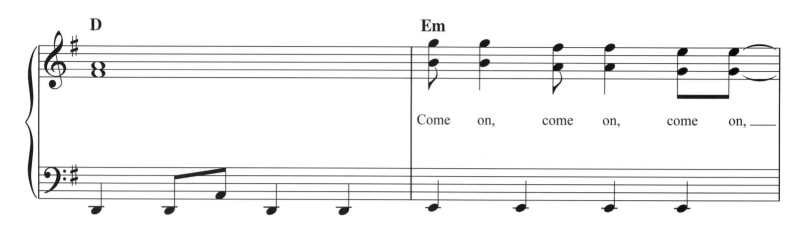

Come on, come on, come on, ____

____ won't you turn my soul in - to a rag - ing fire?

D.S. al Coda

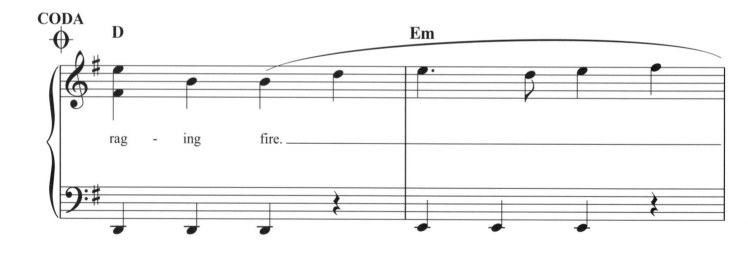

rag - ing fire. ____

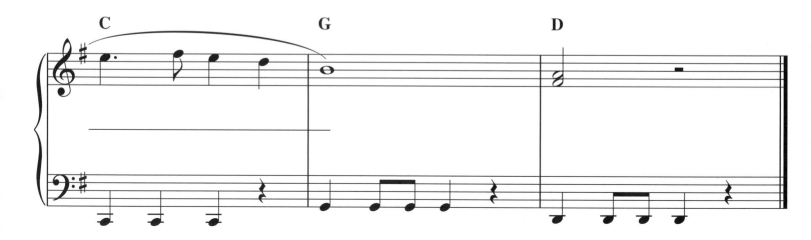

SING

Words and Music by ED SHEERAN
and PHARRELL WILLIAMS

Pop, with a groove

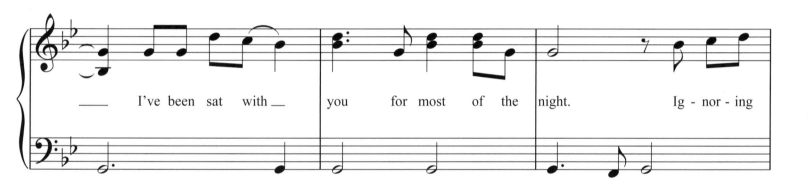

pro-gram. I want you to ___ be mine, la - dy, ___ and to hold your bod - y

close. Take an-oth-er step in-to the no-man's land for the long-est time la - dy. I

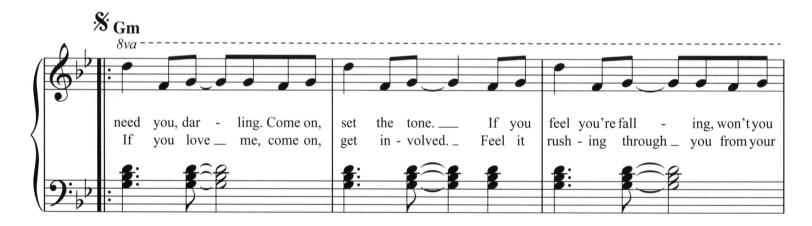

need you, dar - ling. Come on, set the tone. ___ If you feel you're fall - ing, won't you

If you love ___ me, come on, get in - volved. ___ Feel it rush - ing through ___ you from your

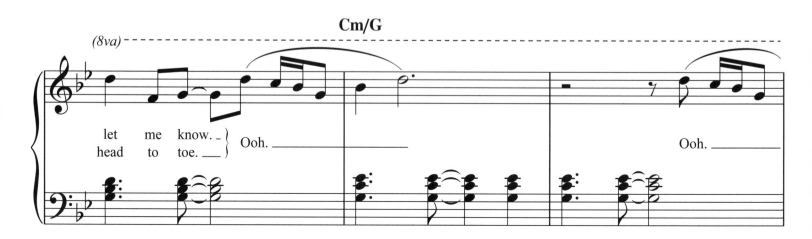

let me know. ___ } Ooh. _____ Ooh. _____

head to toe. ___ }

Gm

blaze. I saw flames from the side of the stage, and the fire bri-gade comes in a cou-ple of days. Un-til

then, we got noth-in' to say and noth-in' to know but some-thin' to drink and may-be some-thin' to smoke.

Cm

Let it go un-til our roads are changed, sing-ing we found love in a lo-cal rave. No,

I don't real-ly know what I'm sup-posed to say, but I can just fi-gure it out and hope and pray. I

Gm

told her my name and said, "It's nice to meet ya." Then she hand-ed me a bot-tle of wa-ter with te-qui-la.

I al-read-y know it, she's a keep-er, just from this one small act of kind-ness. I'm in

Cm

deep, if an-y-bod-y finds out I'm meant to drive home. But I drink all of it, now I'm not.

D.S. al Coda
(with repeat)

So - ber-ing up, we just sit on the couch. One thing led to an-oth-er. Now she's kiss-ing my mouth. I

CODA

Oh. _____ Can you

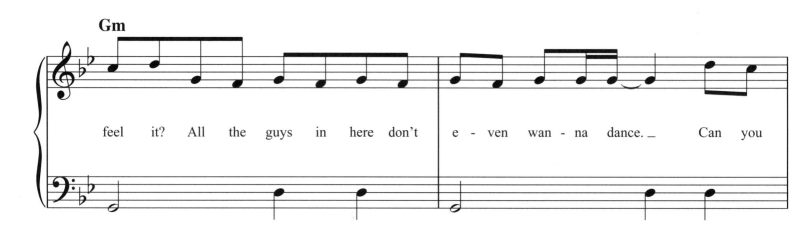

Gm

feel it? All the guys in here don't e - ven wan - na dance. _ Can you

feel _ it? All that I can hear is mu - sic from the back. _ Can you

Cm

feel it? Found you hid - ing here, so won't you take my hand, _____ dar - ling,

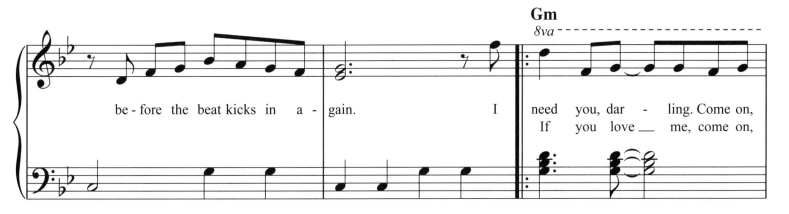

be - fore the beat kicks in a - gain. I need you, dar - ling. Come on,
If you love ___ me, come on,

set the tone. ___ If you feel you're fall - ing, won't you
get in - volved. ___ Feel it rush - ing through ___ you from your

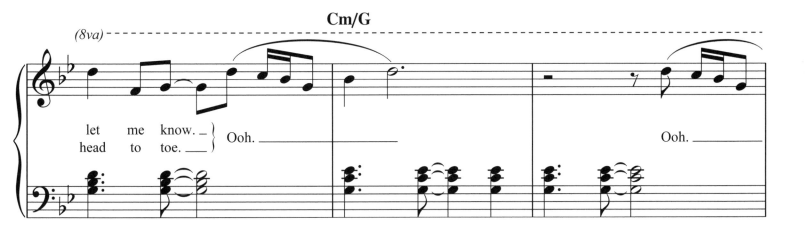

let me know. ___ Ooh. ___ Ooh. ___
head to toe. ___ Ooh.

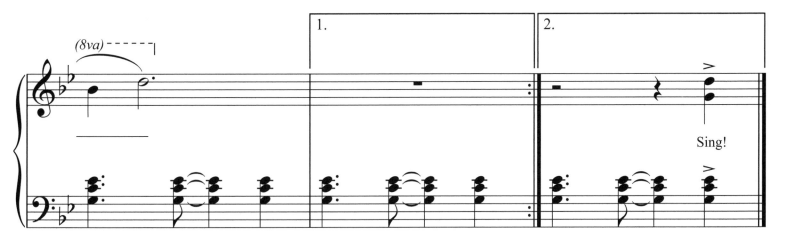

1. 2.

Sing!

STAY WITH ME

Words and Music by SAM SMITH,
JAMES NAPIER and WILLIAM EDWARD PHILLIPS

Moderate Soul

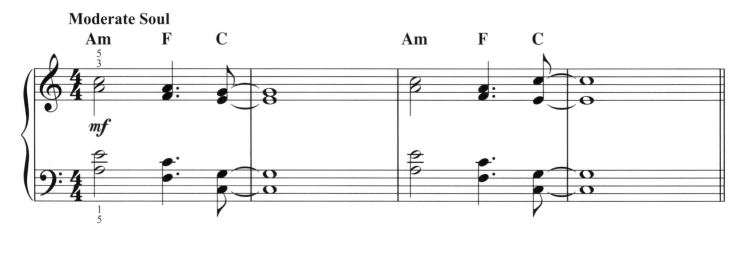

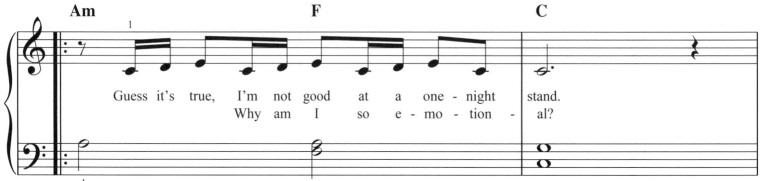

Guess it's true, I'm not good at a one-night stand.
Why am I so e-mo-tion-al?

But I still need love 'cause I'm just a man.
No, it's not a good look. Gain some self-con-trol.

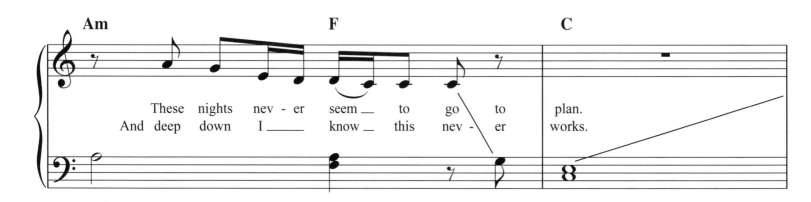

These nights nev-er seem to go to plan.
And deep down I know this nev-er works.

I don't want you to leave, will you hold my hand?)
But you can lay with me so it does-n't hurt.)

Oh, won't you

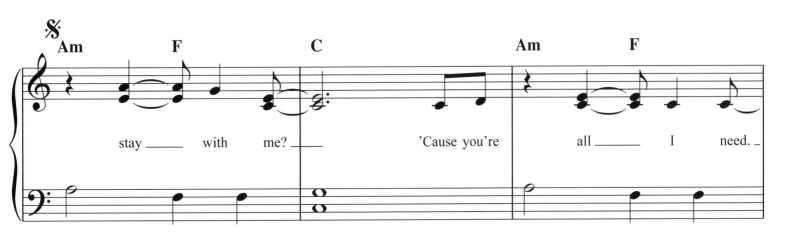

stay with me? 'Cause you're all I need.

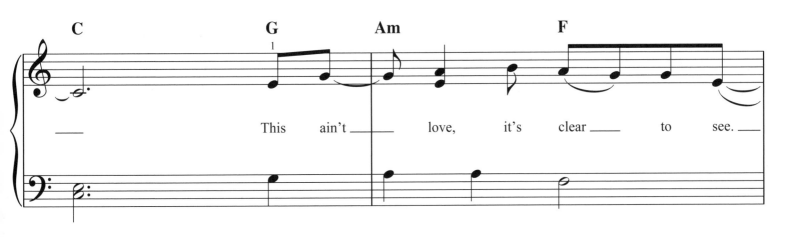

This ain't love, it's clear to see.

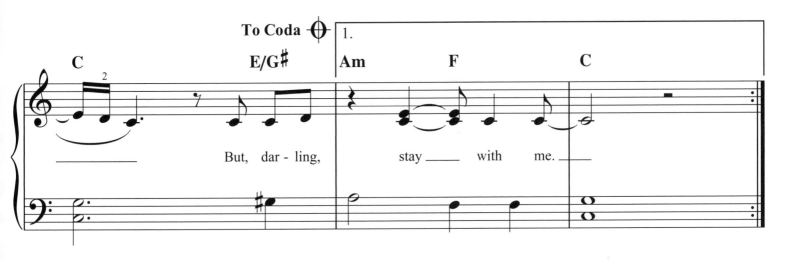

To Coda

1.

But, dar-ling, stay with me.

90

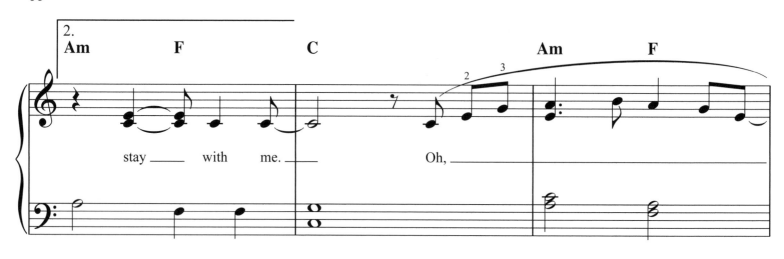

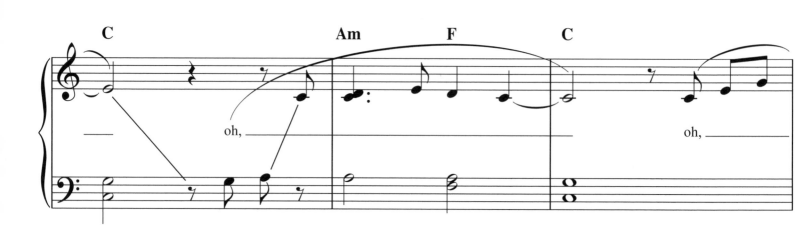

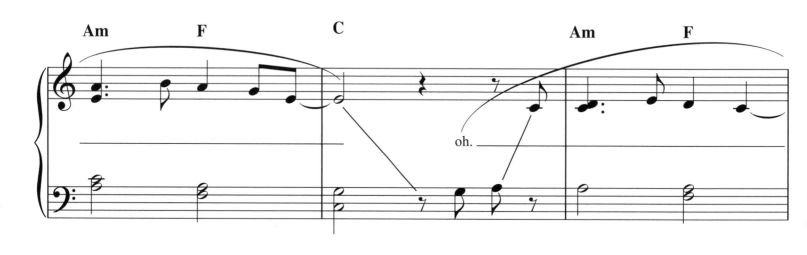

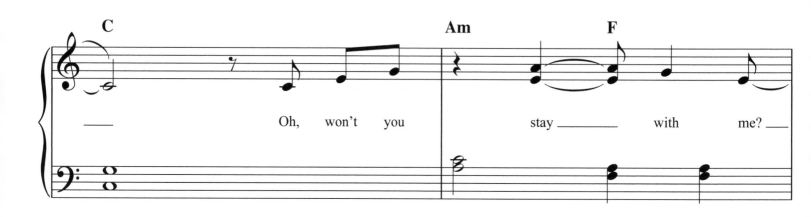

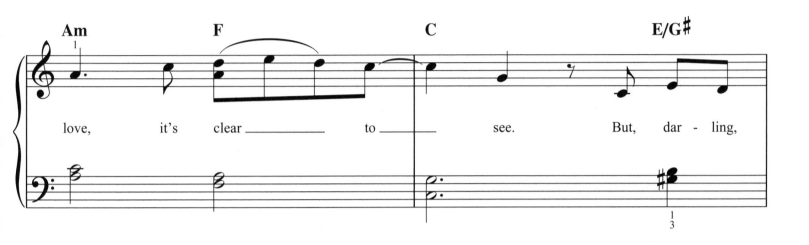

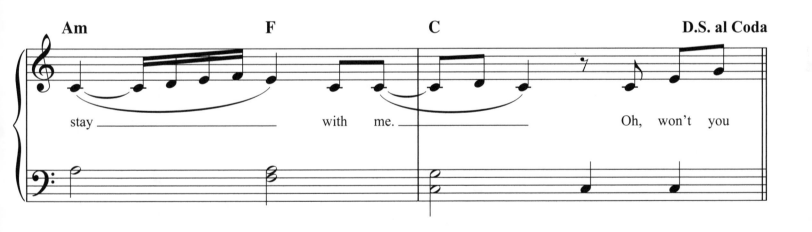

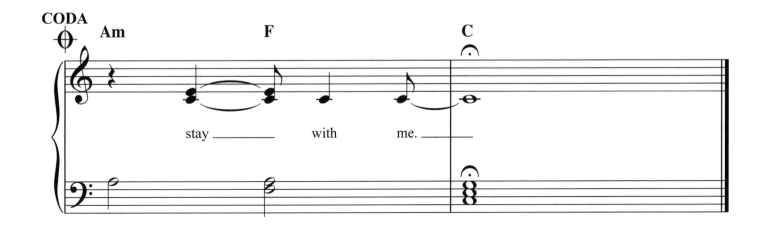

SUMMER

Words and Music by
CALVIN HARRIS

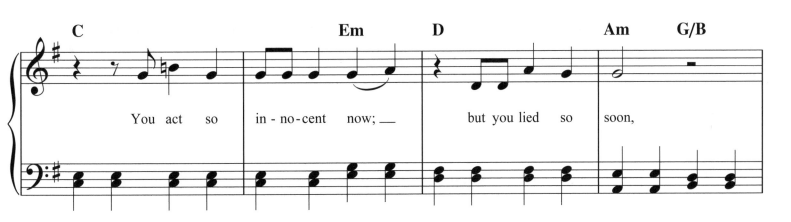

You act so in-no-cent now; ___ but you lied so soon,

when I met you in the sum-mer.

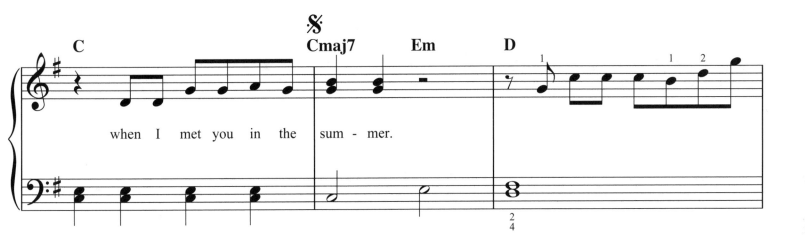

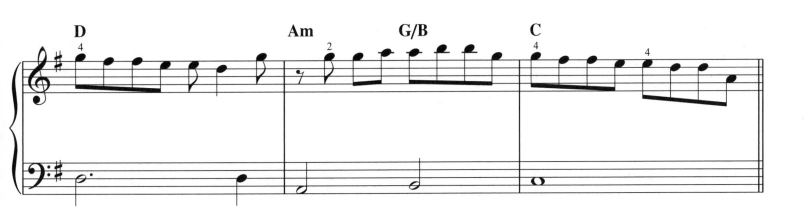

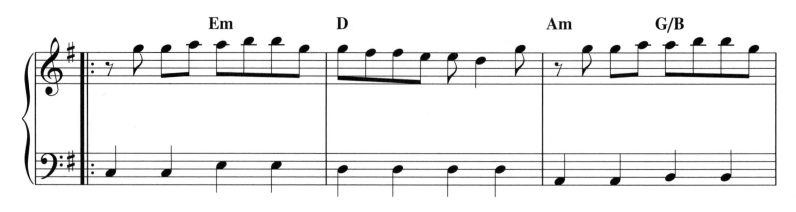

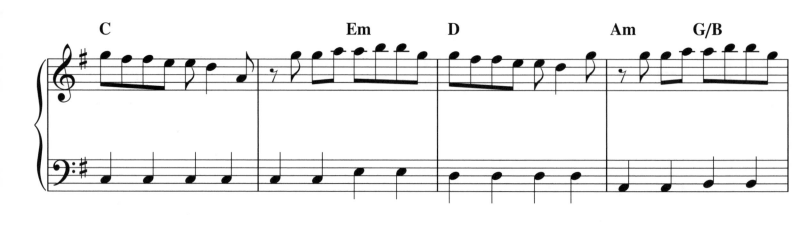

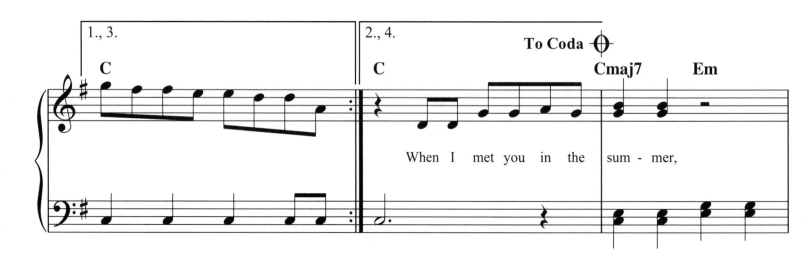

When I met you in the sum - mer,

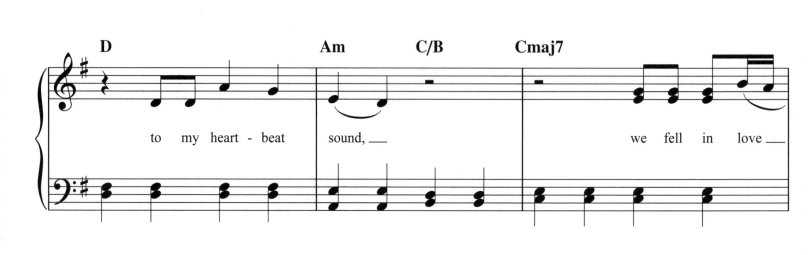

to my heart - beat sound, ___ we fell in love ___

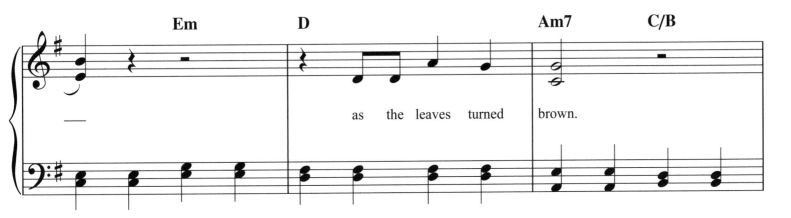

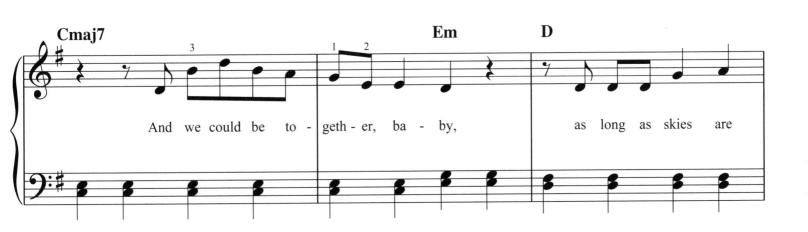

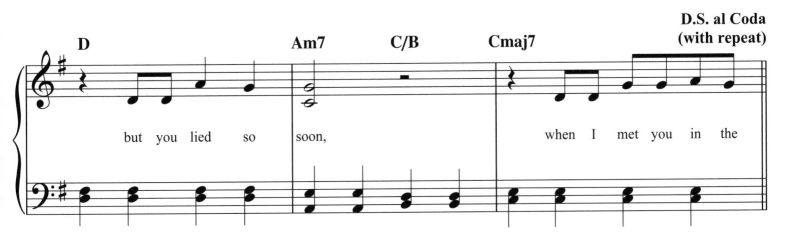

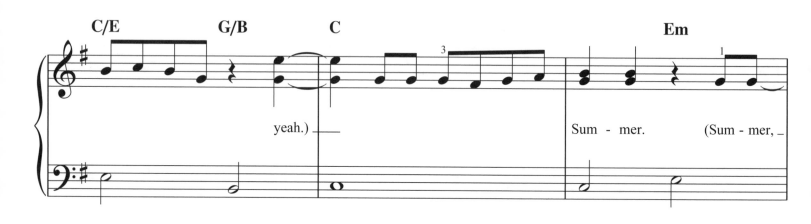

Sum - mer,   yeah.)

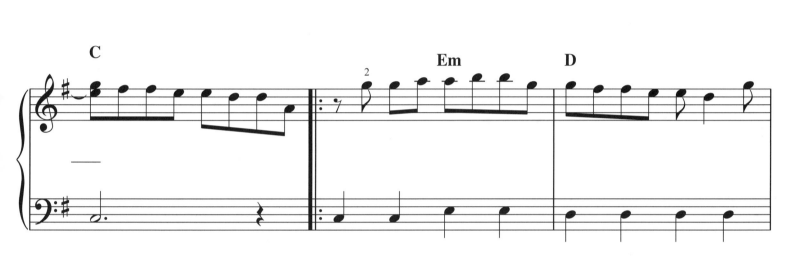

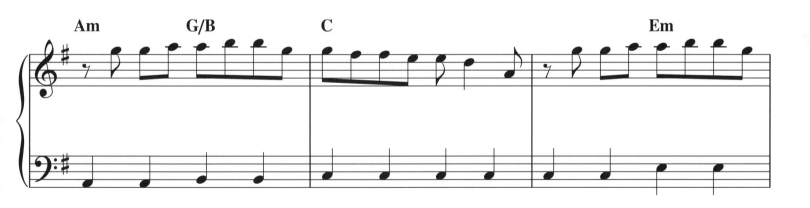

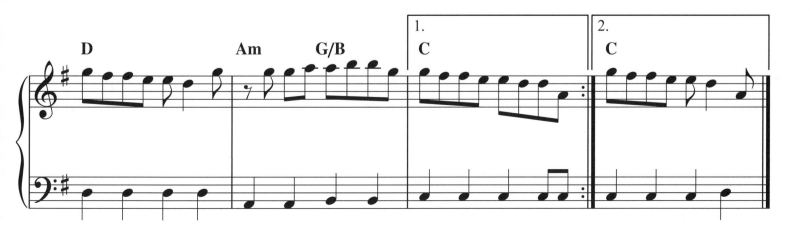

TIMBER

Words and Music by ARMANDO CHRISTIAN PEREZ,
PEBE SEBERT, KESHA SEBERT,
LUKASZ GOTTWALD, HENRY WALTER,
BREYAN STANLEY ISAAC, PRISCILLA RENEA,
JAMIE SANDERSON, LEE OSKAR,
KERI OSKAR and GREG ERRICO

Ooh, _____ ooh, _____ ooh. _____

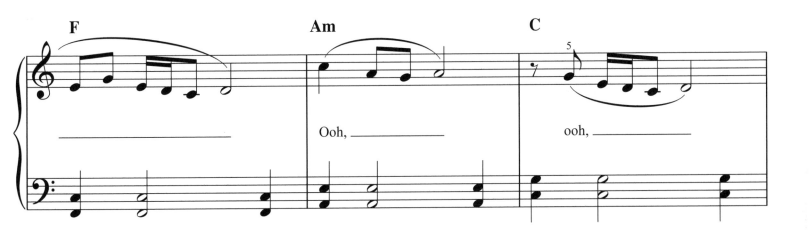

_____ Ooh, _____ ooh, _____

ooh. _____

Rap 1: *(See additional lyrics)*
Rap 2: *D.S.(See additional lyrics)*

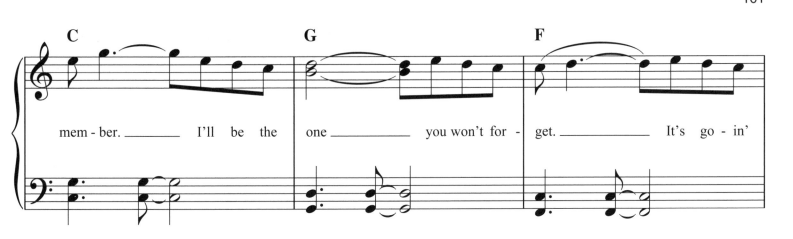

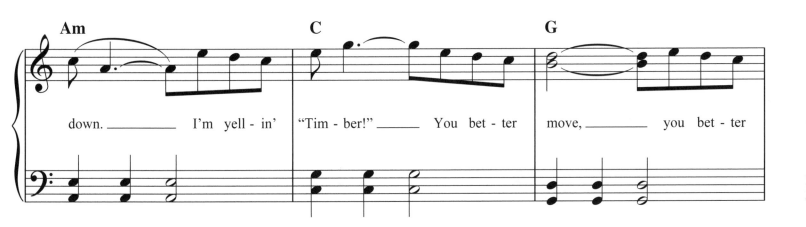

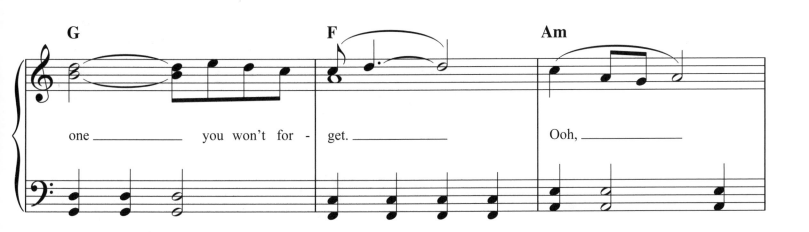

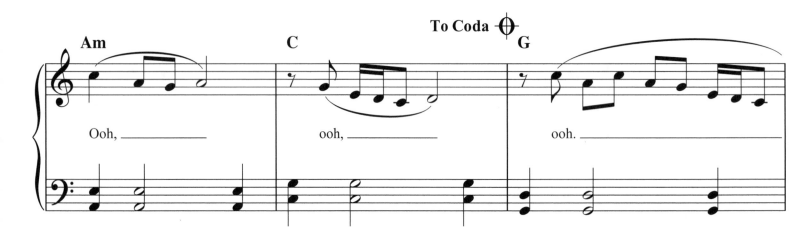

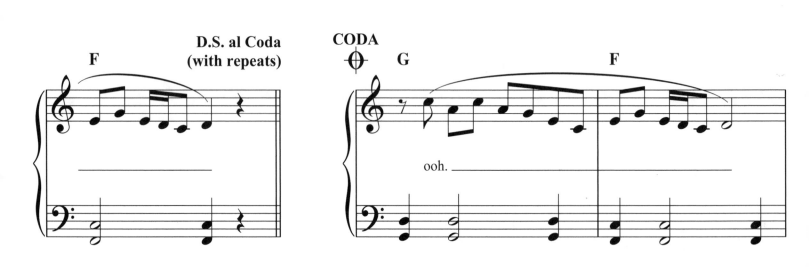

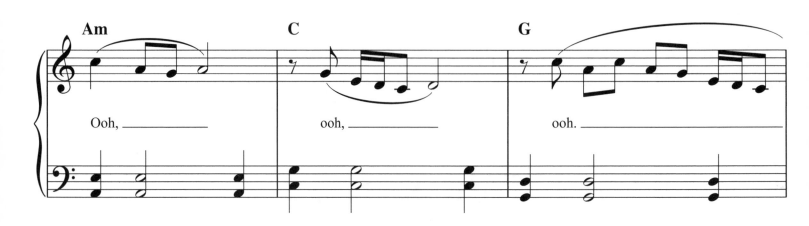

Additional Lyrics

Rap 1: The bigger they are, the harder they fall. This biggety boy's a diggety dog.
Have 'em like Miley Cyrus, clothes off twerkin' in their bras and thongs. Timber!
Face down, booty up. Timber! That's the way we like it. What? Timber!
I'm slicker than an oil spill. She say she won't, but I bet she will. Timber!

Rap 2: Look up in the sky, it's a bird, it's a plane. Nah, it's just me. Ain't a damn thing changed.
Live in hotels, swing on planes. Blessed to say money ain't a thing.
Club jumpin' like LeBron now. Voli, order me another round, homie.
We about to crown. Why? 'Cause it's about to go down.

THE GREATEST SONGS EVER WRITTEN

The Best Ever Collection
Arranged for Easy Piano with Lyrics.

The Best Acoustic Rock Songs Ever

64 songs: Against the Wind • American Pie • Barely Breathing • Change the World • Dust in the Wind • Free Fallin' • Have You Ever Seen the Rain? • I Will Remember You • Landslide • Maggie May • Night Moves • Superman (It's Not Easy) • Tears in Heaven • Yesterday • and more.
00311750.. $17.99

The Best Broadway Songs Ever

85 songs: All I Ask of You • Cabaret • Don't Cry for Me Argentina • Getting to Know You • If I Were a Rich Man • Luck Be a Lady • Memory • Ol' Man River • People • Younger Than Springtime • and many more!
00300178.. $21.99

The Best Children's Songs Ever

102 songs: Alphabet Song • The Ballad of Davy Crockett • Bingo • A Dream Is a Wish Your Heart Makes • Eensy Weensy Spider • The Farmer in the Dell • Frere Jacques • Hello Mudduh, Hello Fadduh! • I'm Popeye the Sailor Man • Jesus Loves Me • The Muffin Man • On Top of Spaghetti • Puff the Magic Dragon • A Spoonful of Sugar • Twinkle, Twinkle Little Star • Winnie the Pooh • and more.
00310360.. $19.95

The Best Christmas Songs Ever

69 of the most-loved songs of the season: Auld Lang Syne • Blue Christmas • The Christmas Song (Chestnuts Roasting on an Open Fire) • Feliz Navidad • Grandma Got Run Over by a Reindeer • Happy Xmas (War Is Over) • I'll Be Home for Christmas • Jingle-Bell Rock • Let It Snow! Let It Snow! Let It Snow! • My Favorite Things • Old Toy Trains • Rudolph, The Red-Nosed Reindeer • Santa Claus Is Comin' to Town • Toyland • You're All I Want for Christmas • and more.
00364130.. $19.95

The Best Contemporary Christian Songs Ever

50 songs: Awesome God • El Shaddai • Give Me Your Eyes • I Can Only Imagine • Live Out Loud • Only Grace • Place in This World • Testify to Love • Voice of Truth • and dozens more.
00312086 Easy Piano $19.99

The Best Country Songs Ever

78 songs, featuring: Always on My Mind • Could I Have This Dance • Crazy • Daddy Sang Bass • Forever and Ever, Amen • God Bless the U.S.A. • I Fall to Pieces • Jambalaya • King of the Road • Love Without End, Amen • Mammas, Don't Let Your Babies Grow Up to Be Cowboys • Paper Roses • Rocky Top • Sixteen Tons • Through the Years • Your Cheatin' Heart • and more.
00311540.. $17.95

The Best Easy Listening Songs Ever

75 songs: And I Love You So • Blue Velvet • Candle on the Water • Do You Know the Way to San Jose • Don't Cry Out Loud • Feelings • The Girl from Ipanema • Hey Jude • I Write the Songs • Just Once • Love Takes Time • Make the World Go Away • Nadia's Theme • One Voice • The Rainbow Connection • Sailing • Through the Years • Unchained Melody • Vincent (Starry Starry Night) • We've Only Just Begun • You Are So Beautiful • and more.
00311119.. $19.99

The Best Gospel Songs Ever

74 gospel songs, including: Amazing Grace • Blessed Assurance • Do Lord • Give Me That Old Time Religion • How Great Thou Art • I'll Fly Away • Just a Closer Walk with Thee • More Than Wonderful • The Old Rugged Cross • Precious Lord, Take My Hand (Take My Hand, Precious Lord) • Turn Your Radio On • The Unclouded Day • When the Roll Is Called up Yonder • Will the Circle Be Unbroken • and many more.
00310781.. $19.95

The Best Hymns Ever

116 hymns: Amazing Grace • Beneath the Cross of Jesus • Christ the Lord Is Risen Today • Down by the Riverside • For the Beauty of the Earth • Holy, Holy, Holy • It Is Well with My Soul • Joyful, Joyful We Adore Thee • Let Us Break Bread Together • A Mighty Fortress Is Our God • The Old Rugged Cross • Rock of Ages • Were You There? • and more.
00311120.. $17.95

The Best Jazz Standards Ever

71 jazzy tunes: Ain't Misbehavin' • Bye Bye Blackbird • Don't Get Around Much Anymore • Easy to Love • The Girl from Ipanema • It Don't Mean a Thing (If It Ain't Got That Swing) • The Lady Is a Tramp • My Funny Valentine • The Nearness of You • Old Devil Moon • Satin Doll • Stardust • Tangerine • and more.
00311091.. $17.95

The Best Movie Songs Ever

71 songs: Alfie • Beauty and the Beast • Born Free • Circle of Life • Endless Love • Theme from *Jaws* • Moon River • Somewhere Out There • Speak Softly, Love • Take My Breath Away • Unchained Melody • A Whole New World • and more.
00310141.. $19.95

The Best Praise & Worship Songs Ever

74 songs: Agnus Dei • Better Is One Day • Come, Now Is the Time to Worship • Days of Elijah • Firm Foundation • God of Wonders • Here I Am to Worship • I Can Only Imagine • Jesus, Lover of My Soul • Lamb of God • More Precious Than Silver • Open the Eyes of My Heart • Shine, Jesus, Shine • There Is a Redeemer • We Bow Down • You Are My King (Amazing Love) • and more.
00311312.. $19.99

The Best Rock Songs Ever

More than 60 favorites: All Shook Up • Born to Be Wild • California Dreamin' • Duke of Earl • Free Bird • Great Balls of Fire • Hey Jude • I Love Rock 'N Roll • Imagine • Let It Be • My Generation • Na Na Hey Hey Kiss Him Goodbye • Oh, Pretty Woman • Rock Around the Clock • Spinning Wheel • Takin' Care of Business • Under the Boardwalk • Wild Thing • and more.
00310444.. $17.95

The Best Songs Ever

71 must-own classics: All I Ask of You • Blue Skies • Call Me Irresponsible • Crazy • Edelweiss • Georgia on My Mind • Imagine • Love Me Tender • Moonlight in Vermont • My Funny Valentine • Piano Man • Satin Doll • Tears in Heaven • Unforgettable • The Way We Were • When I Fall in Love • and more.
00359223.. $19.95

HAL•LEONARD®
CORPORATION
7777 W. BLUEMOUND RD. P.O. BOX 13819 MILWAUKEE, WI 53213
www.halleonard.com

Prices, contents, and availability subject to change without notice. Not all products available outside the U.S.A.

0913